Medieval
Goldsmith's Work

Medieval Goldsmith's Work

Isa Belli Barsali

Paul Hamlyn

LONDON · NEW YORK · SYDNEY · TORONTO

Translated by Margaret Crosland from the Italian original
L'Oreficeria Medioevale
© 1966 Fratelli Fabbri Editori, Milan
This edition © 1969
THE HAMLYN PUBLISHING GROUP LIMITED
LONDON · NEW YORK · SYDNEY · TORONTO
Hamlyn House, Feltham, Middlesex, England
Text filmset in Great Britain by
Yendall & Co. Ltd., London
Printed in Italy by
Fratelli Fabbri Editori, Milan

Art historians and critics of today have now abandoned, except on a limited practical level, the distinction between arts considered to be 'major' and 'minor' or applied; and, even on a practical level, the borderlines are often ill-defined.

The artistic category with which this book is concerned, namely the work of the goldsmith, is a case in point. Sometimes it may be considered as a branch of sculpture, as far as its plastic or monumental achievements are concerned; but in other instances—Limousin, Mosan and Rhenish enamelling of the Romanesque period—it belongs to painting. This validity of goldsmith's work on various levels is apparent not only when we examine the production of a great master, but also when the narrative interest prevails over the merely decorative one, as it tends to during the Middle Ages from the Carolingian to the Gothic period, and, when human or animal figures and symbols are concerned, expression is achieved through sculpture, not in true statues, but in reliquary busts, or in parts of ciboria, dossals and frontals destined for altars.

Goldsmith's work moreover makes use of certain techniques and processes which also belong to full-scale sculpture. There is in effect only a difference of size between casting a large work in bronze and a small object in gold or silver. What is more, after casting, both types of work have to be 'finished' by treatment with punch, chisel and polishing. Thus one can say that if some goldsmith's work can be regarded as sculpture, equally some works of sculpture come very close to the products and creations of the goldsmith: Andrea Pisano, Ghiberti and Filarete chiselled their great bronze doors piece by piece, working on a minute scale. This fact becomes more immediately obvious when metal which is not prized by sculptors is set with jewelled work in gold and silver (for example, in monumental Byzantine doors), or broad gilded plaques so that the work might look as though it were gold; and in the same way the 'Paradise door' in the Florentine baptistery, revealed Ghiberti as a great goldsmith.

It was not only the Renaissance that produced artists able to handle gold, bronze, marble and wood all with the same degree of mastery. Nicholas de Verdun and many other German goldsmiths of the 12th and 13th centuries were in reality great sculptors. The creator of the plaques with figures on an enamelled ground, in the Museo Nazionale in Pisa, was certainly a sculptor belonging to the circle of Nicola Pisano; while at the beginning of the 14th century, in the inscription on the pulpit of the Duomo in Pisa, Giovanni Pisano proclaimed himself as a sculptor in stone, wood and gold. For him, as for many other medieval artists, and for men like Pollaiuolo or Cellini later, limitations, whether of materials, dimensions or style, did not restrict their capacity and power of expression.

It could be said that, of all arts, that of the goldsmith requires the greatest number of patient manual and instrumental operations, and of precise ideas which need to be continually renewed. Patience and precision is demanded in working out the structural and decorative design, in the preparation of materials and tools and in the execution and finishing of the work, while metallurgical and chemical experience is needed in order to choose the most suitable process, and to prevent the work of many months being wasted.

The many technical processes known to have been used in the Middle Ages, which are mentioned briefly here, were inherited from the Classical world, enriched by the experience of the Barbarians, and re-elaborated through day-to-day experience. The working of gold and silver, but also of copper—which has similar ductility and malleability—and of bronze, included various phases.

Once the design was worked out, it had to be cast. The goldsmith had to possess the modelling capacities of a sculptor, and also precise knowledge of the

1. Parcel gilt silver reliquary. End of the 4th century.
Milan Cathedral.

2.   Silver plate with a bird (possibly a parrot?). Sassanian.
6th century. Ny Carlsberg Glyptotek, Copenhagen.

1.   Parcel gilt silver reliquary. End of the 4th century. Milan Cathedral. The scenes from the New Testament on the sides and the cover show Hellenistic influence in their soft relief and in the figures' freedom of movement within the space. This is one of the most obvious examples in which Classical vocabulary and formal beauty have been transferred to Christian themes.

2.   Silver plate with a bird (possibly a parrot?). Sassanian. 6th century. Ny Carlsberg Glyptotek, Copenhagen. Sassanian work, especially on silver plate and vessels for table use, is among the most splendid and imaginative ever produced. Zoomorphic motifs occur frequently and, by way of Byzantine, Syrian and Arab art, last until the Middle Ages in the West.

3.   Eagle in filigree and granulated gold with gems. Byzantine. 6th century. Nationalmuseum, Stockholm. The formal treatment and the strong pose give this truly outstanding jewel a vigorous symbolic value.

3. Eagle in filigree and granulated gold with gems.
Byzantine. 6th century. Nationalmuseum, Stockholm.

behaviour of refractory materials, as well as a knowledge of waxes if the *cire perdue* method were being used. The object could also be constructed by working and mounting sheets of metal foil of varying thicknesses. These were treated by the embossing method, which consisted of executing the design in relief, working with a hammer on the reverse side, proceeding at the same time to reshape it by correcting the changes in the metal; or by using the low relief method, working on the outside face by means of a small blunt scalpel. For these operations the plate was fixed on a suitable support which had to be elastic and pliable and was made of wood, tin or pitch.

If the same decorative motif had to be repeated several times, for example in necklaces, pectorals, borders etc., moulds were used. A punch of iron or bronze was prepared, and pressed directly on to the thin sheet of gold or silver, or else a soft matrix was made, usually of lead. In all types of manufacture, whether embossed or cast, centre punches made it possible to carry out minute incisions and work, while a chiselling process achieved the refinement of details by means of a whole series of instruments (chiselling irons and punches) of widely differing shapes and quality which the goldsmith manufactured for himself. Among the tools used are flat and curved grainers, rectangular and square planes, the outliner for making corner edges, the cross-cut chisel, the groover, the pearler and various types of scrapers.

Several decorative methods were used during the manufacturing process. In filigree work the fine threads were cut out from the edge of a sheet or disc, and finished with a hammer or by the cold stamping process, or else drawn through a draw-plate and twisted or waved. Granulation consisted in soldering on to the surface of the object a spray, or granules of gold, by means of a technique which has not yet been definitely reconstructed. Further processes were those of adding patina, gilding or silvering by means of plaques, or by the use of heat and gouache, inlay, enamelling, incrustation with gems, the use of sections in rock crystal and hard stones. Processes experienced vicissitudes of fashion: openwork found great favour with the Germanic peoples after the 6th-7th centuries, and the effects obtained by inlay were also used, while filigree, for instance, or jewelled creations were more popular among later goldsmith's work.

A goldsmith was almost always an expert not only in all these techniques but was also fully a master of them even though enamelling and the handling of jewels required their own specialists.

BYZANTINE PRODUCTION

Byzantine jewellers, like those of Rome, preferred the use of fine gold leaf to large-scale materials; they also employed discreet quantities of gems: pearls from the Indian Ocean, lapis lazuli from Asia Minor, variegated agates, rose quartz, emeralds and amethysts. This led to an essentially chromatic mode of expression to which was added the use of enamelling, niello work, incrustation, along with various alloys of greenish, pinkish or yellow gold. The courtly and grandiose taste of Byzantine civilisation expressed in its architecture and painting, its ceremonial robes and furnishings, was also reflected in the art of its goldsmiths.

The earliest work belongs to the end of the 4th and to the 5th centuries and possesses a definitely classical vocabulary. Later the style becomes more purely linear, the representation of the human figure tends to disappear—although it is retained in the enamelled sections—and a fanciful range of ornament is used. Here Sassanian influence is apparent in bracelets with leaf and griffin designs and memories of Roman models survive in some armlets with small golden globules at the prominent points of the design. Other armlets, more typically Byzantine, were made in the shape of bands and truncated cones, entirely enamelled, with animal figures and stylised vegetable motifs framed between tracery and gold seed-pearls. The two splendid 9th-century pieces in the Archaeological Museum in Thessalonica, are good examples of the Byzantine type.

Earrings of this period, which often hung down to the shoulders, included enamelling, pearls and precious stones; in necklaces, pearls and unevenly cut emeralds can be seen together; rings assumed considerable dimensions and were sometimes decorated

4.　Earring. Byzantine. Between 659 and 688. Museo
Archeologico Nazionale, Naples.

4.   Earring. Byzantine. Between 659 and 688. Museo Archeologico Nazionale, Naples. This earring is one of a pair worked in cloisonné pastes from the excavations at Senise (Potenza). The woman's head which appears on each pendant is treated in a summary, purely decorative fashion.

5.   Gospel cover with the Archangel Michael. Byzantine. 11th century. S. Marco, Venice. The refined linear stylisation and the classical harmony of composition, the studied treatment of the chromatic surrounds and the hieratic unearthly quality of the figure combine to make this work one of the best examples of Byzantine art. The various techniques used, embossing and chiselling, filigree and granulation, mounted stones and enamelling, reveal an exceptional mastery and technical craftsmanship.

6.   Pala d'Oro (Golden altarpiece). Byzantine and Italian. 10th-14th centuries. S. Marco, Venice. The Pala d'Oro is as glittering an example of the goldsmith's art as the icons it frames are of the painter's. It was put together in 1345 by Giampaolo Boninsegna from enamelwork brought to Venice from Constantinople as plunder by the Crusaders of 1204.

5.   Gospel cover with the Archangel Michael. Byzantine. 11th century. S. Marco, Venice.

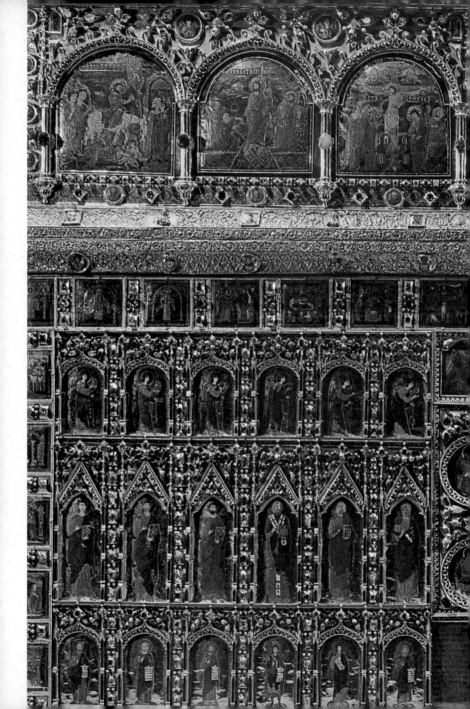

with gaudy stones or with a gold boss incised with figurative designs. The Byzantine goldsmiths also adopted openwork (called by the Romans *opus interrasile*), and the effects of contrast which they achieved became a characteristic of their style; but above all their work is notable for its formal stylisation and emblematic vigour.

Line and colour, reduced to essentials and indeed on the point of dissolving into pure decoration, are the principal stylistic vocabulary of the late 7th-century earring at the Museo Archeologico Nazionale in Naples. Similar elements are to be found in the more complex representation of the Archangel Michael on the cover of the 11th-century Gospel in the Treasury of S. Marco, Venice. Here the customary chromatic technique of the enamel is rendered still more exquisite by the predominating greens and blues, either with dots of pure white standing out clearly on the dark sleeve, or in the subtle designs of the wings, with contrasts between colour and gold; the large areas of gold and the embossing produce an effect of greater richness. The light reflected from the clear planes of the face makes it stand out from the background, which is minutely worked in filigree and seed-pearls, giving hieratic dignity to the figure and an aura of the supernatural. On an embossed silver plaque of the 11th or 12th centuries, which shows the Holy Women at the tomb, and was part of a Gospel cover (Louvre, Paris), the subtle vibration of the chiaroscuro, enlivened by a swift-moving fluid line, defines the design of the elongated figures

6.   Pala d'Oro (Golden altarpiece). Byzantine and Italian. 10th-14th centuries. S. Marco, Venice.

and maintains the decisive diagonal movement in an equilibrium that was typical of the Byzantine 'second golden age'.

The mosaic pictures of the two Imperial courts in the church of S. Vitale at Ravenna provide documentary evidence on goldsmith's work in church furnishings by the jewelled cross of bishop Maximilian and the richly worked book cover and censer of his assistants; but these mosaics also offer an interesting display of the jewels in use during the 6th century and indeed for a long time thereafter. Justinian wears a circular crown with horizontal rows of precious stones, and a huge jewelled fibula; the two ministers have gold curved fibulas, and the soldiers wear large gold necklaces. In the mosaic opposite, Theodora wears a diadem ornamented with gems and two pendants which hang down on to her bosom, mingling with her long earrings; around her neck is a necklace of emeralds and gold (there is a similar one in the Metropolitan Museum of New York, but it is decorated in addition with pearls); over her shoulders and breast hangs a great collar made of fabric embroidered with gold, precious stones and pearls, in a manner derived from oriental fashions. The Empress's ladies also wear long polychrome earrings, necklaces and bracelets; and the last lady on the right is conspicuous with her diadem of green and white stones.

We accept without question today that the value of an object lies in its artistic and antiquarian qualities and is not determined by the splendour and value of the metals used. But, and this is not only true of antique objects, the rarity and intrinsic value of the metals, in conjunction with changes of taste, has meant that the major part of the production of each generation of goldsmiths gradually disappeared to be melted down again in the crucibles of their successors. Nearly all the antique Byzantine jewellery that remains has been found in excavations on the outer fringes of the Empire, either to the north or in Asia Minor: these 'hoards', which were buried to protect them from raids by nomadic tribes or Arabs, often include coins, which simplify the problem of dating. Mock jewellery, in gilt bronze and silvered metal, made as a precaution against theft, has also been found.

In ceremonial furnishings and apparel the Imperial court, as the most important buyer, exerted its full influence. In addition to openwork, enamelling and stone-setting, embossed work, especially in silver, was very widespread. Embossed work reflects classical influences, and silver dishes in particular take up pagan themes again; as early as the beginning of the 5th century, the pictorial sensitivity and softness of the Hellenistic style of modelling were already being replaced by a linear type of stylisation and formal simplification which tended to rely on the contour alone in its treatment of figurative subjects.

The range of products was very varied—silver and gold serving-dishes, gold plates decorated with scenes of the Emperor and episodes from his reign, golden thrones with gilded canopies supported on columns, furniture worked and encrusted with gold and silver

8. Gold necklace. Nordic-Germanic. First half of the 6th century. Statens Historiska Museum, Stockholm.

7. Gold medallion. Nordic-Germanic. 6th century. Statens Historiska Museum, Stockholm.

9.   Detail of the necklace illustrated in Plate 8.

7. Gold medallion. Nordic-Germanic. 6th century. Statens Historiska Museum, Stockholm. Germanic art absorbed Oriental elements from the Scythians, the Sarmatians and the Huns, and combined them with others derived from the Celts and the Roman traditions. In 6th-century work human figures can be seen along with interlacing motifs. Sometimes, as in this object which comes from Gerete (an island in Gotland) the figures are of Classical derivation but renewed by a fresh interpretation.

8. Gold necklace. Nordic-Germanic. First half of the 6th century. Statens Historiska Museum, Stockholm. Three golden circular necklaces, coming from Västergotland, are among the oldest productions of Nordic goldsmith's work. In this one, which comes from Alleberg, the three rigid circles joined together are filled out by means of coils and spirals in filigree work. The necklace was fastened by means of a pin-hinge at the back of the neck and a dovetail joint in front.

9. Detail of the necklace illustrated in Plate 8. The movement and vibration of light on each single circle are heightened not only by the particular type of coil arranged alternately with the filigree (a very widespread technique in Scandinavia) but also by a dense mass of masks and human and animal figures.

10 Gold fibula with precious stones. Germanic. 5th-6th centuries. Nationalmuseet, Copenhagen. The fibula comes from the princely tomb of Aarslev on the island of Fyn; it is the arched type and is distinguished by its curvilinear shape and by the filigree and granulation treatment which follows and emphasises the setting of the stones. The contacts between Scandinavian and oriental goldsmith's work were very close.

10. Gold fibula with precious stones. Germanic. 5-6th
centuries. Nationalmuseet, Copenhagen.

plaques, and the decorative gold plaques used on sarcophagi such as the one made for Justinian which Corippus describes. Probably the most remarkable products of the Byzantine goldsmiths were the automata used in the elaborate court ritual stage-managed and designed to overawe visiting embassies. The incredible richness of apparel and jewels exalted the Emperor to a superhuman sphere, and in the hieraticism of the ceremonial the unearthly glow of goldsmith's work echoed the sacred nature of the monarchy. The Imperial court also made rich gifts to the churches of Constantinople not only of vestments but also of furniture such as silver- or gold-mounted bejewelled candelabra or golden lamps which hung down in clusters. Of course the Imperial largesse was lavished most profusely on the great church of Hagia Sofia. The capitals of the columns were covered with Justinian's gold; the doors were covered with sheets of silver and gold and various alloys; the choir, the seats, the patriarch's throne were also covered with gold and silver foil and studded with pearls and various types of garnet; the golden altar, surmounted by the silver ciborium and then, above, by the vast dome decorated only with a gigantic cross, was the centre of magnificent liturgical ceremonies. The profusion and glittering colours of the goldsmith's work overwhelmed all thought of terrestrial realities and created a hypnotic impression of the divine presence. Paulus Silentiarius, describing the church on the occasion of the second consecration in 562, said: 'In the evening so much light was reflected

28

from the temple that you would have thought it to be a midnight sun . . .'

Whereas the secular and domestic products of the Byzantine goldsmiths have largely disappeared as a result of the intrinsic value and rarity of the materials, proportionately more has survived of the rich church furnishings, both because of their value as part of the ecclesiastical patrimony as well as their sacred nature.

Crosses, patens, chalices and reliquaries in precious metals were enriched by a profusion of jewels, enamelling and pearls; and extremely fine Gospel covers were made, like those given to Hagia Sofia by Justinian, with gold foil, gilded and enamelled silver, precious stones and pearls. Yet over the years the treasures of the Church sustained great losses. The Iconoclastic period of the 8th and 9th centuries saw the destruction of many fine pieces and the barbaric sack of Constantinople by the Fourth Crusade, in 1204, destroyed countless treasures of all kinds.

The new forms and techniques evolved by the Byzantine goldsmiths were copied in the West and provided it with models throughout the medieval period. Indeed, many objects of liturgical furnishing today still retain the shapes given them by Byzantine master-craftsmen. The new techniques included the interesting juxtaposition, in the same object, of embossed and filigree work on, for example, collets and enamelled plaques, a juxtaposition which lent itself to an infinite number of expressive possibilities. New styles of decoration included the introduction of brilliant cloisonné enamel on to small plaques carry-

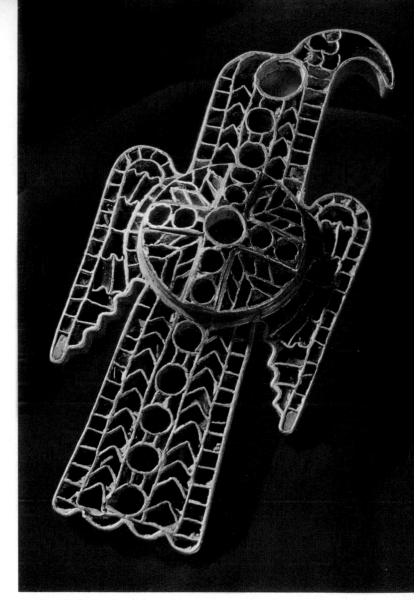

11. Fibula in the shape of an eagle, made of gold and precious stones. Ostrogothic. End of the 5th century. Germanisches Nationalmuseum, Nuremberg.

12. Crows set with gems. Ostrogothic. 3rd
century. Römisch-Germanisch Museum, Cologne.

11.   Fibula in the shape of an eagle, made of gold and precious stones. Ostrogothic. End of the 5th century. Germanisches Nationalmuseum, Nuremberg. The central disc embodying a cross and the cells, of varying shapes, make up the decorative geometrical motifs. Originally the cells contained flat carved stones, worked in a style found throughout the whole Germanic world; fibulas fairly similar to this one, from Cesena, have been found in Spain.

12.   Crows set with gems. Ostrogothic. 3rd century. Römisch-Germanisch Museum, Cologne. These examples of goldsmith's work come from the territory in southern Russia where the Goths built their empire and whence they descended on western Europe.

13.   Temporals in curled shapes made from gold set with precious stones. Ostrogothic. 5th century. Römisch-Germanisch Museum, Cologne. In these objects, which come from the area of Gothic settlement in Russia, the filigree work and the precious stones create a geometrical type of decoration with oriental motifs and taste.

13. Temporals in curled shapes, made from gold set with precious stones. Ostrogothic. 5th century. Römisch-Germanisches Museum, Cologne.

ing representations of people. Among the various novelties introduced into church furnishings was the modification of the reliquary from the older type of solid box-like container to one in the form of a cross or a triptych, within which the relics could be clearly seen by the faithful.

Towards the end of the 6th and the beginning of the 7th century the Imperial workshops in Constantinople increased in number; the interest of the court in the art of the goldsmith is clear from the fact that even an Emperor, Constantine VII Porphyrogenitus (911-959) did not think it beneath him to give up part of his time to it. The collection of pieces plundered by the Crusaders in 1204, and now in the treasury of S. Marco in Venice, offers a comprehensive survey of the achievements of the Byzantine goldsmith's art. Enamelled reliquaries, magnificent Gospel covers, great two-handled chalices with semicircular cups of onyx, sardonyx and agate or rock crystal and gold mounts incrusted with gems and minute enamelled medallions, and finally the collection of enamels which during the 14th century were mounted together in the composition of the most dazzling 'Pala d'Oro' of the Middle Ages.

The art of the goldsmith in the Italian peninsula, was dominated by the Graeco-Roman tradition, especially in embossed and chiselled work. This tradition was absorbed in timely fashion by the Christian artists of the 4th century so that elements of the classical vocabulary of themes survived in later production. The parcel-gilt silver reliquary case from the altar of the church of the SS. Apostoli (later S. Nazaro Maggiore) in Milan clearly derives from Greek models. The composition of the figures, their free and harmonious movement in space, the fluid linear movement and the soft chiaroscuro modelling, all enable us to assign it to the end of the 4th century, the period of the first consecration of the church.

Rome, together with Milan, remained a great artistic centre even after the fall of the western Empire. The *Liber Pontificalis* gives information about the production in gold, although most of the pieces disappeared subsequently in the devastations to which the city was subjected. Originally, for example, the font in the baptistery of St John Lateran was decorated with statues of gold and there were arches of silver over its ciboria; at the time of Pope Honorius I (625-638), a shining gold door stood in the façade of the Vatican basilica with the figures of the two Roman apostles. The vessels and chalices studded with gems and worked in chiselled plates, and the openwork of this period, could easily hold their own in comparison with contemporary Byzantine goldsmith's work.

In the 8th and 9th centuries Byzantine forms came to predominate in Roman goldsmith's work, even though this was necessarily influenced by the strong opposition to iconoclastic doctrines in western Christianity. The effect of works produced in Rome during this period was of monumental sculpture carried out in precious metal. The church of Sta Maria Maggiore had a statue in gold of the Madonna and Child, dating from the time of Pope Stephen II (752), that of S. Paolo fuori le Mura had a Christ between two angels in silver; the basilica of the Vatican had stands decorated with silver images of Christ with the Apostles and Mary with the ten virgins, attributable to the reign of Pope Gregory III (731-741); an image of St Andrew in gold and gems stood in the oratory of S. Andrea near St Peter's; while under Paschal I (817-824) silver statues of the Saviour and of the saints Processus and Martinian were executed for the chapel dedicated to them.

Roman churches, for example Sta Prasseda, S. Giorgio al Velabro and Sta Maria in Trastevere, had altars or ciboria glowing with silver foil coverings, which were often gilded; the silver in the ciborium of St 'Agata dei Goti weighed 720 lb; the covering in gold plates carried out by order of Leo III (795-816), was said to be 453 lb; and at the order of Adrian I (771-795) the magnificent golden lamp in the shape of a cross carrying 1465 candles was made in Rome for the church of St Peter. Valuable gifts from the Byzantine court had already arrived in the West, sent to popes, kings and churches. Justinian I had given Pope Hormisdas (514-523) vessels of gold and silver, Gospels with precious bindings of gold and jewels, a paten in gold with oriental jacinths and two others in silver, as well as two small golden coffers. Two gifts which reached Rome from Byzantium are today in the Museo Sacro in the Vatican: the oval capsella (probably early 6th century and listed in the *Sancta Sanctorum*) made from embossed

14. Fibula in the shape of a bee, and earring. Ostrogothic.
5th century. Germanisches Nationalmuseum, Nuremberg.

15. Helmet with clasps, made from bronze, partly gilded, with silver plaques. Merovingian. 5-6th centuries. Altertumsmuseum, Mainz.

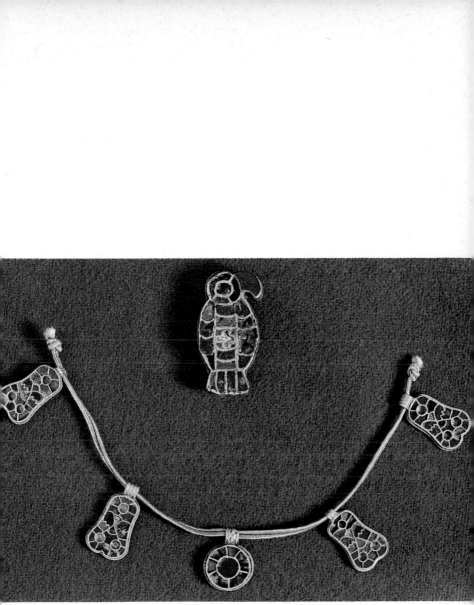

16. Zoomorphic fibula and necklace with pendant ornaments. Merovingian. 7th century. Museo Archeologico, Cividale.

14.　Fibula in the shape of a bee, and earring. Ostrogothic. 5th century. Germanisches Nationalmuseum, Nuremberg. Decorative polychrome work is fairly common among the products of Ostrogothic goldsmiths. It is found either in geometrical or naturalistic designs, an example of the latter being the characteristic bee-shaped fibulas.

15.　Helmet with clasps, made from bronze, partly gilded, with silver plaques. Merovingian. 5th-6th centuries. Altertumsmuseum, Mainz. From the royal tomb at Planig. Barbarian arms are often richly decorated, for example sword-grips may be of gold ornamented with precious stones set in cloisonné style, with clasps and finishings for straps.

16.　Zoomorphic fibula and necklace with pendant ornaments. Merovingian. 7th century. Museo Archeologico, Cividale. These two pieces represent the contrast between the extreme simplification of the decorative range and that taste for chromatic effects so popular with Germanic goldsmiths.

17.　S-shaped fibulas in gold, set with precious stones in cloisonné. Merovingian. 7th century. Museo Archeologico, Cividale. The S-shaped fibulas found in northern Italy date both from before and after the Lombard invasion (569) and appear in various forms. In one of those illustrated the two-headed dragon motif appears; the theme was widespread during the 7th century in the Scandinavian area, England, Gaul, Austria and Italy. In the other example the animal heads have become pure arabesques.

17. S-shaped fibulas in gold, set with precious stones in cloisonné. Merovingian. 7th century. Museo Archeologico, Cividale.

silver and with a jewelled cross on the cover and busts of the saints between shields; and the cross given by the Emperor Justin II (565-578) with a Latin inscription and praying figures of the Emperor and the Empress. About 569 Justin also sent a small reliquary of the True Cross to Ste Radegonde in Poitiers.

The style and themes of Byzantine goldsmith's work spread throughout the East and West; its influence was vast and profound in matters of technique and iconography and also from the aesthetic point of view. Although this is not the place for a detailed examination of its various aspects some must be noticed: the high degree of craftsmanship and refinement in the work, the vast extent of the cultural and commercial ties between East and West, the authority of the church in Constantinople and the weight and political prestige of the Empire. At Monte Cassino, the mother church of the order of St Benedict, were to be found images in embossed silver, bronze candlesticks and an enamelled altar frontal, all of which are examples of Byzantine goldsmith's work.

An account of medieval European goldsmith's work which omitted the vast stylistic influence of Byzantine art would be a very distorted one, and this is true not only for the products of Barbarian times but also for the achievements of the Carolingian, Ottonian and Romanesque period, to which Byzantine art made a fundamental contribution.

BARBARIAN GOLDSMITH'S WORK

When we review the artistic development of Europe between the 4th and the 10th centuries, the most obvious phenomenon is the clear-cut and profound difference to be seen between classical and late antique art on the one hand, and early medieval art on the other. Within this broad distinction a further one must be observed, that between pagan and Christian art. On the one hand the style is irrational and disassociated, on the other harmonious and rationalistic, on the one hand abstract or incongruous, on the other deriving from organic nature.

The fact is that alongside and outside the artistic civilisation of classical tradition—Graeco-Roman and Hellenistic-Byzantine—other cultures had been developing, the Barbarian civilisations, of which the most important were the Celtic, Germanic and Scythian. And during the transition period between the late antique and the early medieval worlds, this group of Eurasian civilisations experienced vast movements of populations and cultures.

During these migrations, destructive as they were, the main directions of medieval cultural and social development were nevertheless established. Germanic civilisation, whose centre shifted from East to West as a result of the migration of the peoples, came closer to the regions already subjected to the Roman Empire through economic, religious and cultural links. The final demarcation between East and West was to some extent determined by the expansion of the Arabs which began in 635 with the conquest of Syria and aggravated the separation of the West from the countries of the East. In the following centuries a diversity of causes extended the axis of Europe towards the north from its previous centre in the Mediterranean. The result was a Latin-Germanic bloc, bordered on the Atlantic and the Mediterranean by Celtic and Slavonic areas in the process of being absorbed, while the North Sea tended to become the new internal sea. In the forms and substance of its artistic expression, this vast area shows differing conceptions, with diverse and non-interchangeable languages; but we also find these languages co-existing in complicated interrelationships, so that the various traditions modified and consolidated one another. Through its multifarious and complex contacts with the older and richer civilisations, the Barbarian tradition saw various changes in vocabulary, morphology and syntax and accepted new technical, iconographic and stylistic traditions. Gradually the bases and postulates of classical civilisation, in their turn, modified and stimulated by Barbarian art, which was itself undergoing a transformation, became an increasingly important and eventually a fundamental part of the emerging civilisation of medieval Europe.

Goldsmith's work remains the principal evidence of the art of the Barbarian people. But it is not easy to set out and analyse the framework of the decorative motifs, technical methods and types, which vary between a protohistorical range and obvious oriental

18. Circular tray with hen and chickens in silver gilt.
Lombard. 6th century. Monza cathedral.

19. Cross of Agilulf. 6th century. Monza cathedral.

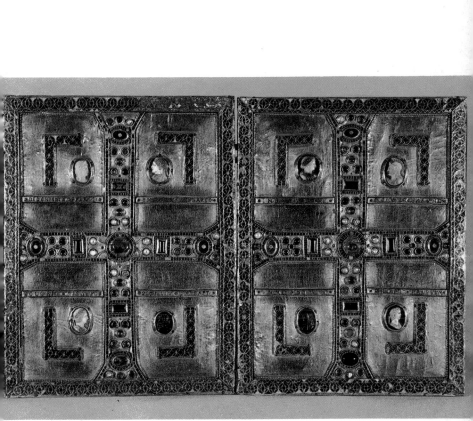

20. Gospel cover. Late 6th or early 7th century. Monza cathedral.

18.   Circular tray with hen and chickens in silver gilt. Lombard. 6th century. Monza cathedral. According to some experts this unusual piece symbolises the seven provinces into which the Lombard kingdom was subdivided; according to others it is a symbol of fecundity. It probably dates from the time of Theodelinda, who is said to have presented it to the cathedral of Monza.

19.   Cross of Agilulf. 6th century. Monza cathedral. Byzantine art had considerable influence in the West during the Middle Ages; this piece probably came from a Roman workshop. Much of its beauty derives from the juxtaposition of the blue and green stones with the iridescence of the pearls and the long pendants. The front and back of the cross are both decorated in the same way.

20.   Gospel cover. Late 6th or early 7th century. Monza cathedral. This extremely refined work, probably Roman in execution, was given by Pope Gregory the Great to the Lombard Queen Theodelinda in 603. The classical clarity of the design is mingled with gems and antique cameos, between mounts and designs of precious stones set in cloisonné.

21.   Gold fibula, embossed work, with filigree and precious stones. Lombard. 7th century. Museo dell' Alto Medioevo, Rome. This work, which comes from the cemetery of Castel Trosino, shows a taste which is still deeply permeated by Byzantine influence. The interlace design follows the line of Mediterranean tracery, alternating regularly with the embossed parts which contain bezels holding flat stones.

21. Gold fibula, embossed work, with filigree and precious
stones. Lombard. 7th century. Museo dell' Alto Medioevo,
Rome.

origins. The Gothic peoples, for instance, who were among the first to settle in Italy, reveal, in addition to elements from Byzantine culture, influences from Sarmatian and Scythian art. Only a map of the migrations and areas of settlement can give an idea of the spread and interrelationship of motifs and processes. Apart from the continuation of the classical tradition in some form or another, the very mobility of the migrants obviously forms a limit to any reconstruction of the artistic areas and their influence.

The art of the Germanic peoples was essentially decorative but it is probable that the animal motifs it employed had a symbolic, possibly a magical significance which is now lost. Zoomorphic ornamentation is characteristic of the goldsmith's work of the Scandinavian and Anglo-Saxon Nordic peoples. It retains derivations from the art of the steppes, either through indirect links or through the migrations of the Huns, and probably spread towards northern Europe either along the Danube or up the so-called northern route which the Goths used in their migration southwards from Russia.

One of the most outstanding examples, both of this ornamentation and of Scandinavian goldsmith's work, is provided by the necklace dating from the first half of the 6th century coming from Alleberg and now in the Statens Historiska Museum in Stockholm. A formal vocabulary which is wholly independent of the classical tradition is expressed in the dense and vibrant mass of minute animal forms, men and human masks. The effect is enriched by filigree work and the coiled bands which give formal articulation to the three circlets of the necklace. The underlying abstract tendencies of this theme assume important evidence in the representational compositions with quadrupeds and beasts of prey which occur in many clasps and fibulas. An example is the 6th-century Nordic-Germanic medallion also in the Statens Historiska Museum in Stockholm. The iconographic theme derived from Roman coinage is translated throughout the medallion in terms of two-dimensional space, and becomes a sybilline decoration combining a horse and a human head; the triangle emerging with the six masks in high relief develops on the other hand that diverse and autonomous vocabulary already seen in the Alleberg necklace.

It is difficult to trace the origins of the technically superb filigree work found in Scandinavian pieces. Among the German peoples it can be seen already in the first centuries of the post-classical era, and would appear to take over from classical art the use of ox-head motifs and hanging ornaments in the shape of Roman vessels. Groups of animals with extended bodies woven into fantastic designs, which form a characteristic motif in much of the goldsmith's work of Lombardy appear widely in Anglo-Saxon pieces and are found later in Irish art. Outstanding examples can be seen on the treasure from the Sutton Hoo ship-burial, dating from the first half of the 7th century, and now in the British Museum, London;

particularly fine are the fibula and purse-cover in ivory and gold. On the latter object there are also two symmetrical pairs of animals, and the symbolic motif, repeated twice, of the pairs of animals facing a human figure, which was already present in similar stylised forms in pieces of Nordic-Germanic gold-smith's work.

Another characteristic feature of Anglo-Saxon products was the use of polychrome decoration expressed in the network at the edging, linked with red almandines but also with glass pastes in the *millefiori* style.

The stones are rounded and each one mounted on an isolated collet, or else worked flat and mounted in geometrical cells covering the entire object. Their colour had already played a dominating part in Barbarian goldsmith's work, beginning with the splendid gold finds from the treasury of Petroasa (National Museum, Bucharest), of uncertain ethnic origins but dated to the second half of the 4th century, and then in the fibulas in the shape of eagles or bees or the S-shaped designs typical of the Ostrogoths which occur in Italy between 489 and 553. The two methods of working and using the stones can be seen in Ostrogothic jewels of the 5th century, such as the earrings and temporals in the Römisch-Germanisches Museum in Cologne and the eagle in the Germanisches Nationalmuseum in Nuremberg.

The same practice of covering the whole decorative surface with jewels is followed in Lombard circular fibulas. These are formed from a cloisonné network

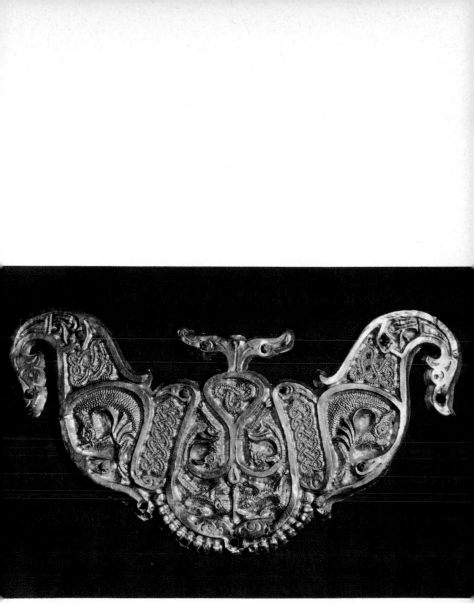

22. Saddle ornament in laminated gold. Lombard. 6th-7th
centuries. Museo dell'Alto Medioevo, Rome.

23. Gold fibula. Anglo-Saxon. First half of the
7th century. British Museum, London.

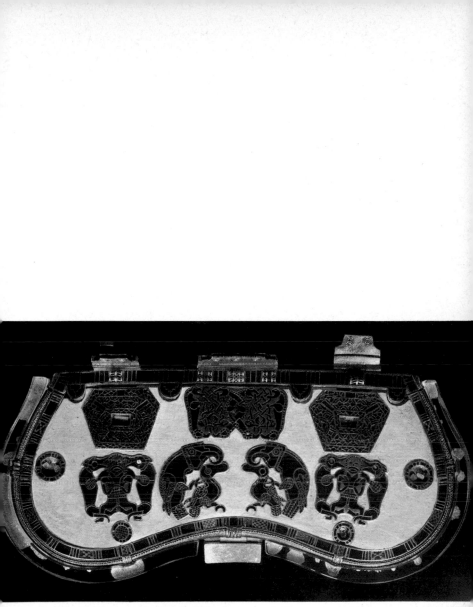

24. Purse cover in ivory with mount and plaques in gold and stones set in cloisonné. Anglo-Saxon. First half of the 7th century. British Museum, London.

22.   Saddle ornament in laminated gold. Lombard. 6th-7th centuries. Museo dell'Alto Medioevo, Rome. This magnificent piece, found at Castel Trosino, shows an organic, composite design combining Mediterranean tracery elements and Byzantine-style lions and griffins; the textures and division of the framework reveal Germanic taste.

23.   Gold fibula. Anglo-Saxon. First half of the 7th century. British Museum, London. From the Sutton Hoo ship burial excavated in 1939. The zoomorphic interlace design, asymmetrical but perfectly balanced and punctuated with niello work, covers the entire decorative surface of the object.

24.   Purse cover in ivory with mount and plaques in gold and stones set in cloisonné. Anglo-Saxon. First half of the 7th century. British Museum, London. The finds at Sutton Hoo provide evidence of the imagination, the iconographic vocabulary and the technical mastery of the Anglo-Saxon goldsmiths. As well as the zoomorphic designs on some of the plaques there are figurative motifs of animals and of Daniel in the Lions' Den; along with the precious stones set in cloisonné there is enamel work of the type usually called *millefiori*.

25.   Pastoral staff in silver. Irish. 11th century. National Museum of Antiquities of Scotland, Edinburgh. Ireland was not touched by the Roman and Germanic invasions; the indigenous Celtic culture accepted and developed the process of conversion to Christianity. The shape of this pastoral staff is reminiscent of a horse's head; at the end of the handle is a small reliquary.

25. Pastoral staff in silver. Irish. 11th century. National Museum of Antiquities of Scotland, Edinburgh.

consisting usually of curved lines matching each other with a certain degree of symmetry, the base being formed from a sheet of gold leaf which has been scratched in order to increase the scatter of reflected light through the stones. With this type of setting (for example, in the circular fibulas taken from Imola and Parma) there can also be found a decorative fillet used in the place of cells and precious stones, usually the red almandines or garnets employed over the very wide Germanic area north of the Alps, and—as we have already seen—as far afield as the Anglo-Saxon area of the British Isles, and some Visigothic regions in Spain. From this latter area came the fibulas in the shape of eagles, and those 7th-century royal crowns which are related to those of the Hun period, to Ostrogothic jewellery produced in Italy, and also to Byzantine goldsmith's work.

After the Gothic conquest and the Byzantine reconquest by Justinian in 553, Italy was invaded in 569 by the Lombards. The new conquerors, who established powerful dukedoms, penetrated practically throughout the entire peninsula, and continued the patronage of the valuable goldsmith's work, both Byzantine and Germanic in style, for trinkets or ornaments for belts, clothing, armour or harness for horses. Armour also was richly decorated: gilt bronze panels ornamented shields, gold panels embellished leather quivers or saddles, for example the magnificent saddle ornament from Castel Trosino, now in the Museo dell'Alto Medioevo in Rome.

Unlike the Germanic peoples of northern Europe,

who cultivated their native style with its tendency to the abstract and its own decorative morphology, those of southern Europe, i.e. the Lombards in Italy and the Visigoths in Spain, were heavily influenced by their contacts with Byzantine art and with Coptic art from Egypt. They revealed such a capacity for assimilation and such sensitivity towards the new forms that they could almost be called artistically bilingual. Furthermore, by the very act of occupation the conquering tribes in southern Europe established progressive links with the subject peoples and came to understand their language and culture, religion and way of life.

Certainly the Lombards brought linguistic motifs from central and northern Europe into the Italian peninsula. But at the same time some forms which are non-Germanic or possess a clearly Byzantine accent can be explained as the work of indigenous artists and reveal that the Lombards themselves were able to acquire new artistic forms and adapt themselves to using them.

The treasury of Monza cathedral, although depleted of some of its pieces, can still give an idea of the variety of shapes and styles under the Lombards. According to Paulus Diaconus, the 8th-century historian of the Lombards, Queen Theodelinda had decorated the original basilica of S. Giovanni Battista 'in marvellous fashion with many ornaments of silver and gold'. A 13th-century bas-relief in the lunette over the great door to the cathedral, shows her in the act of offering a crown and a cross to St John the

Baptist, while alongside the lunette itself is a display of the objects which had been donated. Some of them certainly date from the time of Theodelinda—a Gospel cover, a circular crown with horizontal rows of precious stones (partly replaced in the 18th century with mother-of-pearl), a comb with filigree and jewels, a fan, and a hen with chickens in silver-gilt. The objects in this group—others belong to various periods—are clearly not all of the same quality nor of the same type of work.

The hen with chickens cannot be attributed to any definite school or centre; it is an exceptional object of which there are no other examples, and certain stylistic motifs suggest that it is 6th-century work. It may have been a gift to bring good luck, for the Lombards regarded the hen as a symbol of fecundity. Other objects breathe the atmosphere of traditional Byzantine culture. An example is the exceptional Gospel cover illustrated in plate 20. A border, grained with a network of cloisonné rings, encircles a cross which is edged with stones and a row of seed-pearls, and ornamented with pearls, cabochons of rubies, emeralds and sapphires. The harmonious and rhythmic quality is striking, as is the 'classical' sense of the spacing; this is still more evident in other objects, such as the crosses in Lombard style, for example, the great cross of Desiderius, today in the Museo Cristiano at Brescia. According to a tradition that could well be true the Gospel cover was given to Theodelinda by Pope Gregory the Great in 603, and was made in Rome, a notable centre of goldsmith's

26. Reliquary of the Gospel of St Molaise. Irish. First quarter of the 11th century. National Museum of Ireland, Dublin.

26. Reliquary of the Gospel of St Molaise. Irish. First quarter of the 11th century. National Museum of Ireland, Dublin. Known under the name of 'Soichel Molaise', this is a Gospel cover, signed by the goldsmith Gilla Biathin. On the front cover the symbols of the Evangelists are arranged between the arms of the cross and enclosed between intersecting bands which represent the extreme geometric stylisation of the motif used in the decoration of the sides.

27. Small cross in silver gilt and filigree. Viking. 10th century. Statens Historiska Museum, Stockholm. This crucifix from Birka is the most ancient known to have been made in Scandinavia and displays outstanding technical craftsmanship. The stylisation of the human figure is typical of Viking goldsmith's work.

28. Collar. Viking. 10th century. Nationalmuseet, Copenhagen. In this solid gold collar the ornamentation with closely interwoven bands which are continually knotted and unknotted is fairly characteristic of Viking art.

29. Circular silver fibula. Viking. 10th century. Statens Historiska Museum, Stockholm. One of the circular fibulas found at Gärdslösa, on the island of Öland. Four masks are interspersed with typical animals, their bodies consisting of intertwined shapes, firmly linked together in the form of a cross in the centre and with an interlace design at the edge. The high relief modelling suits the organic nature of the design, and this, in turn, is notably emphasised by the double edging.

27. Small cross in silver gilt and filigree. Viking. 10th century. Statens Historiska Museum, Stockholm.

28. Collar. Viking. 10th century. Nationalmuseet,
Copenhagen.

29. Circular silver fibula. Viking. 10th century. Statens Historiska Museum, Stockholm.

work that was deeply influenced by the culture and taste of Byzantium. The 'classical' coherence of the vocabulary and design of the cover becomes much more evident if one disregards the narrow horizontal bands which were added on Theodelinda's instructions to commemorate the gift, but which are both organically wrong and foreign to the spirit of the work. The cross of Agilulf may be of the same origin: on account of the Byzantine style of the wide open arms, the harmonious arrangement of the gems, the shaded and controlled sense of colour, and the iridescence given to the work by the rows of seed-pearls along the edges.

The outstanding treasures from the Lombard cemeteries of Nocera Umbra, Castel Trosino, Parma, Cividale, Testona and Reggia Emilia include objects of varying taste and of varied cultural components. There are necklaces in which Roman gold coins alternate with glass paste pearls; necklaces of glass grains and pendants of beaten gold; earrings of Byzantine style, mostly in gold, consisting of a large ring and a long pendant ending in pearls; fibulas of all types; brooches, belt buckles and rings.

In addition to these ornaments are crosses of gold leaf, with embossed motifs showing interwoven designs and faces, or more rarely adorned with stones, which were worn as a distinguishing mark by Lombard converts to Christianity. Similar pieces found beyond the Alps are, it has been suggested, the products of the Italian-Lombard workshops and evidence of trading links with northern Italy. From the 8th century these crosses were no longer especially associated with converts and had become generally accepted as jewellery.

The techniques employed—with the exception of the thin cloisonné jewelled plates—are the same as those used in the classical world: casting, embossing, filigree, granulation of gold, openwork, incision of hard stones, raised setting of round-cut stones, and the setting of glass pastes in cells. The technique of inlay also was still used, as can be seen from the 8th- or 9th-century royal folding-stool found in the bed of the river Ticino at Pavia and now in the Museo Civico there; it is made from iron and is inlaid with gold, silver and lead.

The various operations carried out on the one object achieve an immediate and exuberant polychrome effect; chiaroscuro is obtained by the use of embossing and more vibrant results through chiselling and filigree work, and the use of stone and glass pastes. The entire surface of the object is decorated, showing a fear of the 'empty space' typical of European art of this period, and the decorative motifs themselves are animals and interlaced designs characteristic of German taste, although beside typical examples of the confused and boisterous type, there are also flowing, harmonious and regular compositions which reveal a classical origin. Indeed on the small gold crosses made between the end of the 6th and the beginning of the 7th centuries, the animal type of interwoven motif has given way to the more tranquil plaited design. After the 7th century, north of the Alps, the Lombard, Frankish and Burgundian goldsmith's work begins to show also plant motifs which are variations on the classical acanthus, with palm leaves and vines, revealing links with the Byzantine workshops on the Mediterranean.

The numerous surviving fibulas offer a great variety in design. Worn by both men and women, they were used to fasten a cloak in front, or in pairs to secure a full-cut tunic on the shoulders, following a fashion of Celtic origin. In the 7th century in Italy they were commonly made in an S-shape, representing a two-headed monster of Asiatic origin (such as those found at Cividale), and in a circular shape with stone and filigree on a flat background, like the one from Senise in the Museo Archeologico in Naples. Fibulas were also made from embossed metalwork with filigree, cabochon shaped stones and thin plates of cloisonné stones, like the one from Castel Trosino at the Museo dell'Alto Medioevo in Rome. There are a great number of curved fibulas—those from Cividale, for example—mostly in bronze gilt, but also cast in silver and chiselled, with sections either gilded or studded with gems, or decorated with cloisonné stones and glass pastes.

Naturally, in addition to variations in type, there is variation in quality. Compare for instance two circular fibulas: the one from Senise is a diligent and calligraphic piece of filigree work on one plane; the one from Castel Trosino on the other hand shows the use of various techniques for the achievement of an organic and vital decorative texture. In an outer band four embossed studs alternate with settings of glass pastes, while in the centre a gem is surrounded with a wheel motif, which is taken up again with a circular embossed band.

In the circular fibulas referred to above, the symmetrical and well spaced decorative motifs are certainly derived from the classical world and, particularly in the Castel Trosino fibula, support the theory that it was made by native goldsmiths. The curved fibulas however are obviously the work of a Germanic craftsman not only because of the agitated interwoven design which covers the various areas, but more particularly because the craftsman could not resist giving the shape—originally Roman—of the fibula a zoomorphic aspect.

To gain a fuller idea of the more coherent and fluid expression possible in this Barbarian art of abstract and non-organic stylisation let us compare the Sutton Hoo fibula and a Viking circular fibula (plates 23, 30). The Sutton Hoo fibula, dating from the first half of the 7th century, has a zoomorphic band with long wave-like motifs which is continued with a pulsating movement and tied in a knot in the middle. In the later Viking clasp made of bronze gilt (Ny Carlsberg Glyptotek, Copenhagen), the intricate geometric design has an unbroken rhythm carried through knots and labyrinthine bands which weave over and under each other. Among the smooth knots of the border every ornamental element originates in and is conditioned by the preceding one, and in its turn generates others, creating an overall

30. Circular fibula in gilt bronze. Viking. 10th century.
Ny Carlsberg Glyptotek, Copenhagen.

30. Circular fibula in gilt bronze. Viking. 10th century. Ny Carlsberg Glyptotek, Copenhagen. The knotted interlace design of the inner area has a relaxed but strict balance, and the surface is enlivened by the vibration of the light reflected from the filigree-work; in the outer area are some typical Mediterranean-type motifs.

31. Front part of the golden altar. Carolingian. First half of the 9th century. S. Ambrogio, Milan. Work on the altar, completed about the year 835, was supervised by a master called Vulvinius whose assured sculptured style is found in the silver back; the embossed gold plates of the frontal are the work of collaborators and the style achieves more vibrant effects of light. In addition to the mastery of technique and the obvious awareness of an sensitivity to early styles, there is an extraordinary understanding of the material, with the result that the splendour of the metals and precious stones becomes an element in the overall balance of the work.

32. 'Iron' crown. Carolingian. First half of the 9th century. Monza cathedral. This crown, like the altar by Vulvinius, is in the Milanese tradition. It shows the same technical mastery and a similar sense of design, while in both works embossing plays a large part.

31. Front part of the golden altar. Carolingian. First half of the 9th century, S. Ambrogio, Milan.

73

32. 'Iron' crown. Carolingian. First half of the 9th century.
Monza cathedral.

effect of ceaseless intertwining dynamic movement.

The best interpreters of this lively style, which, assimilated in various ways, produced highly poetic results in the later art of the European Middle Ages, were in northern Europe, and they included the goldsmiths of the British Isles. Here, after the 7th century, we find a combination of contemporary Scandinavian art and the ancient Celtic tradition; but objects of Christian art had also penetrated from the Mediterranean world to Britain, and there had even been contact with the monasteries of Egypt and Syria. It is usual to find motifs of spiral curvilinear type, or with opposing curves linked together, or else geometric designs of the Greek type. As might be expected, interwoven in the pattern there are quadrupeds and birds with elongated bodies and claws, sometimes of ample and fluid type, sometimes small-scale and insistent.

In Ireland, where these forms lasted longer, objects were worked in filigree, and champlevé (punched enamelling) was also used, a technique introduced through Celtic products. The results have an elegant and calligraphic, linear stylisation, sometimes derived from Celtic and sometimes from Nordic Germanic art.

Few periods or currents during the early Middle Ages can equal the clarity, the fantasy, suitability, and the decorative, if sometimes scholastic 'feel' of Anglo-Saxon and Irish goldsmith's work, which develops a style that is sometimes grave and large, sometimes diverting and witty, but always cursive and immediate. These stylistic characteristics are reflected in the construction of the objects—for instance, the design assumed by the pastoral crozier that was also used to house relics, which shows a stylised horse's head with a mane.

A good example of the Irish style is the Gospel reliquary known as 'Soichel Molaise', in the National Museum of Ireland, in Dublin. An inscription reveals that it was executed between 1001 and 1023 by Gilla Biathin by order of the abbot Cenfaelad, who succeeded St Molaise at the monastery of Devenish, an island in Lough Erne. Within the clear-cut frame defined by the arms of the cross is the dynamic, contorted design—consisting of animals reduced to long strips and tied together—which are brought into relief by the use of various materials. In the four panels are representations of the symbols of the Evangelists which have become mysterious ciphers through the spiral parts, of Celtic origin, and through the transformation of the sides into connecting bands which pull them together and finish off the design.

Another example of 'fine calligraphy' can be found in the upper part of the guard for St Patrick's bell at the Royal Irish Academy in Dublin, which can be ascribed to the years 1094-1121. The interlacing animal design expands in tranquil curves with a formalism which is almost 'floral'. A fluent prose style, opening out sometimes into passages of lyrical expression, distinguishes this Anglo-Saxon and Irish goldsmith's work; the involuted and tortuous quality of contemporary Viking art, although related, remains on the whole alien to it, apart from a few exceptional cases.

The experiments and research of Anglo-Saxon and Irish artists were extremely profitable also for the goldsmith's work in continental Europe: the first examples were brought back to Scandinavia from the Viking raids on the British Isles of the 8th to 10th centuries, but later they spread directly to the continent through the activity of the Anglo-Saxon and Irish missionaries.

THE CAROLINGIAN AND OTTONIAN RENAISSANCE

The range of European goldsmith's work between the 9th and 10th centuries presents coexistent yet divergent means of expression as a result of stylistic and iconographic interchanges. For example, this period which saw the highest peak of Carolingian and Ottonian art was also the time of the spread of Viking art in Scandinavia, an art which followed and developed typically Germanic formulas and expressions of taste.

In goldsmith's work the range of plant and zoomorphic interlace designs increased and became more elaborate, crowded with human and animal figures treated as demoniac and symbolic masks. This art seemed to be entirely pervaded by a multifarious and

33. Reliquary of the tooth of St John, in gold and precious stones. Carolingian. 9th century. Monza cathedral.

34. Berengaria's cross. Carolingian. 9th century. Monza cathedral.

33.   Reliquary of the tooth of St John, in gold and precious stones. Carolingian. 9th century. Monza cathedral. The symbolic and metaphysical values of the gold and jewels form a striking and worthy setting for the relic.

34.   Berengaria's cross. Carolingian. 9th century. Monza cathedral. The richness and effect of great value given by the colouring of the gems seem to reflect still a continuation of Barbarian taste, while the technique of execution, the setting of the gems and the central rosace are some of the elements characteristic of Carolingian art.

35.   Earring in gold filigree. Carolingian. 9th century. Germanisches Nationalmuseum, Nuremberg. The lightness of this filigree work and the skilful arrangement of the design form an excellent example of the high level reached by goldsmith's work during the Carolingian period.

36.   Gospel cover in gold, precious stones and ivory. Ottonian. 10th century. Schatzkammer, Aachen. In goldsmith's work the august character of Ottonian art assumes a measured discipline in layout and decoration. Four stories from the life of Christ are arranged around a Byzantine ivory, between the jewelled frames of the border and the cross.

37.   Cross described as having belonged to the Emperor Lothair. Ottonian. End of the 10th century. Schatzkammer, Aachen. This is one of the most representative products of Ottonian goldsmith's work, together with the cross of Otto and Matilda (Essen cathedral) which dates from the years 973-982 and is probably derived from it. Carved gems and stones with raised claw settings, together with filigree, are combined with filigree gold set with seed pearls and enamelling.

35. Earring in gold filigree. Carolingian. 9th century.
Germanisches Nationalmuseum, Nuremberg.

36. Gospel cover in gold, precious stones and ivory.
Ottonian. 10th century. Schatzkammer, Aachen.

37. Cross described as having belonged to the Emperor Lothair. Ottonian. End of the 10th century. Schatzkammer, Aachen.

mysterious vitality. In the 10th century circular silver fibula in the Statens Historiska Museum, Stockholm, four 'expressionistic' masks are interspersed with typical interlacing animal designs, creating a texture linked together with an arrangement in the shape of a cross; in other pieces of similar style in the same museum the structure of the object sometimes participates in this animal energy.

In 5th-century Gaul, beneath a Celtic cultural substratum which later came partly under Roman influence, the Germanic population of Franks, converted along with Clovis (481-511) to Christianity, gradually consolidated their position in the kingdom. Dating from the 6th century are splendid shield-type fibulas set with precious stones and containing filigree work, while the characteristic polychrome style of the Goths appears, along with the zoomorphic interlace patterns of a type similar to those found in Anglo-Saxon and Irish culture.

The mid-6th century produced the jewels of Queen Arnegonda, which were found at St Denis; among them are the two gold fibulas of shield type covered in cloisonné work, and a large girdle fibula in silver, with gold appliqué, filigree and cloisonné enamel. The spread of Christianity brought a new range and a new decorative vocabulary, especially plant motifs, of Byzantine and oriental origin.

The flowering of creative ability which lies behind the greatness of Carolingian art is symbolised by the figure of Eligius, the leading court goldsmith and medallist to Clotaire II and Dagobert, appointed

Bishop of Noyon in 641, and later venerated as the patron saint of goldsmiths. As a priest he carried out conversions among the Germans and founded churches and monasteries. As a court functionary of Dagobert he was responsible for arranging the increase of the goldsmith's art and the first institutions connected with it. As a *magister* he founded a workshop in Paris, on the Ile de la Cité, which enjoyed success equal with those of Limoges—where St Eligius was born—Metz, Arras, Lyon, Solignac and St Loup at Noyon, while of his pupils, Thille, the Swabian Tituenus, Buchinus and Baudericus are known to us. As is natural, in view of his almost legendary standing as a goldsmith, all the objects which are thought to have been executed during his time have been quite simply ascribed to him. However the major work attributed to him in the past— the throne of gilt bronze called 'the throne of Dagobert', formerly in St Denis and now in the Louvre—can only be dated with difficulty. It may have been an ancient folding seat; its claw-shaped feet indicate remote oriental origins, while it was provided later at another period with a back in openwork; alternatively it is a Carolingian work of the early 9th century connected with the workshop of Aachen.

The Carolingian artistic renaissance, the first sign that a new and united medieval artistic civilisation was arising, was based on and had its background in the *renovatio imperii*—i.e., the establishment of the Frankish empire which was regarded as the revival of the Roman Empire in the West. The architectural programme of Aachen took its inspiration from the Imperial palaces, with the result that the city appeared to the poet Mondoino like the golden Rome which, in its renewed state, was born again to the world.

The design for the Palatine chapel was inspired by S. Vitale in Ravenna, which was the last seat of the Roman Emperor in the West; Charlemagne had an equestrian statue brought to Aachen from Ravenna, as if to symbolise the fact that the Emperor had passed through, while he had columns, capitals and mosaics transferred from Ravenna and Rome. Among the treasures that he left in his will to St Peter's in Rome were two famous silver panels, now lost, representing the cities of Constantinople and Rome.

In reality there was no question of renewal or restoration of the Roman Empire. The new system was neither Barbarian nor Latin in its cultural ethos but was an autonomous development which, like the new languages of Europe, in fact became neo-Latin!

Carolingian goldsmith's work includes processes such as the combination of gold and gems, and expressive Barbarian motifs and techniques. An example of this is found in the highly elegant inter-lacing designs of the cloisonné enamel cross in the two silver panels at the sides of the porphyry tablet on the portable altar at Adelhausen in the Agostiner-museum at Freiburg im Breisgau, dating from about 800, the only one surviving from the time of Charle-magne. But besides such elements deriving from traditional sources there are other varied influences, found in work at the Irish, Anglo-Saxon, Iberian, Frankish, Syrian and Arabian courts and probably the 'Greek' ones in southern Italy and Byzantium, while goldsmith's work of various origins was collected in the Imperial palaces of the Franks.

In 795 Charlemagne captured the treasure of the Avars and transported it to Aachen (it made sixteen cart loads); in 798 he received from Constantinople gifts given by the Empress Irene; Alfonso II the Chaste, King of the Asturias, sent him the booty captured from the Arabs; in 801 the messengers of the Caliph of Baghdad, Haroun al-Raschid, brought him gifts of some objects of inestimable value. Meanwhile foreign goldsmiths—who certainly included some Byzantines—had settled at Aachen and had developed new techniques and new means of expression.

The important new departure in goldsmith's work of the Carolingian period, and the one which was perhaps to prove the most fruitful for future developments, was the reaffirmation of the human figure as a major design element. In works on religious themes it was expressed through the representation of Christ, the Virgin Mary and the saints, and it was stimulated also by the rejection in the West of iconoclastic doctrines. This indicated obvious links with the Byzantine-Christian stream while other signs reveal undeniable links with classical art.

At the end of the 9th century Germanic animal ornamentation, sometimes overweighted with plant motifs of the acanthus-leaf type, makes rare appearances in Carolingian art. Griffins, lions, fish and

38. Gospel cover. Milan. *c.* 1040. Milan cathedral.

39. Cross. Workshop of Roger de Helmarshausen.
c. 1100. Kunstgewerbemuseum, Berlin.

38.   Gospel cover. Milan. *c.* 1040. Milan cathedral. Milan, along with Rome, was one of the major centres of goldsmith's work. The cover carries the name of archbishop Aribert of Intimiano (1018-1045) on the back section.

39.   Cross. Workshop of Roger de Helmarshausen. *c.* 1100. Kunstgewerbemuseum, Berlin. This cross from St Dionysus in Enger (Westphalia) is in laminated gold, with precious stones and pearls with filigree and niello work. On the front part are antique cameos, while on the back are the Agnus Dei and the evangical symbols.

40.   Cover of Sion Gospel. German (or possibly French). 11th-12th century. Victoria and Albert Museum, London. Splendid examples remain of the Carolingian Renaissance in objects which have a liturgical function, especially Gospel covers.

41.   Flabellum in gilt copper. German. First half of the 12th century. Hildesheim cathedral. This liturgical fan can be ascribed roughly to the decade 1130-1140 and provides evidence of the high technical and decorative level reached by the German goldsmiths.

42.   The Gloucester Candlestick. Gilt bronze. English. 12th century. Victoria and Albert Museum, London. This goes back to 1104-1113. The hypnotically seething mass of the design entwined with animals becomes a more highly disciplined type of exuberance.

43.   Crown of the Holy Roman Empire. Ottonian. 10th century. Kunsthistorisches Museum, Vienna. Destined for the coronation ceremony, the crown has a magnificence which is predominantly materialistic and an explicit coronation symbolism. It was made in the German area in about 962.

40. Cover of Sion Gospel. German (or possibly French).
11th-12th century. Victoria and Albert Museum, London.

41. Flabellum in gilt copper. German. First half of the 12th century. Hildesheim cathedral.

42. The Gloucester Candlestick. Gilt bronze.
English. 12th century. Victoria and Albert
Museum, London.

43. Crown of the Holy Roman Empire. Ottonian. 10th century. Kunsthistorisches Museum, Vienna.

peacocks all receive a naturalistic treatment derived from Roman and Byzantine art and with all the inevitable Oriental implications.

The goldsmiths worked in the great cities of the Empire, and in the workshops attached to the monasteries; their patrons included Charlemagne, Louis the Pious, Charles the Bald, princes, dignitaries and prelates—indeed the same circle of people as those who commissioned the architecture, painting and sculpture. A few artists' names have survived, among them Thuotilus of St Gall, Odulfus, the monk of St Riquier, Bernelius and Bernunius, both canons of Sens, and Perpetuus, who founded Angers, but it is not possible to list definite groups of works.

The splendours of Charlemagne's tomb at Aachen have been dispersed or destroyed. All that remains is the so-called 'talisman' found around the Emperor's neck when Otto II caused his tomb to be opened in the year 1000. This is a portable gold reliquary in the shape of a medallion. It has a large transparent sapphire on one side and on the other a glass cabochon, through which the relic can be seen, surrounded with a framework of enamel and filigree, with pearls, garnets and emeralds. The talisman is now in the cathedral treasury at Rheims.

Of the Imperial jewels and insignia there remains only the reproduction of the crown—its jewelled band enhanced by three fleurs-de-lys—which appears on the 9th-century bronze statuette from the treasury of Metz cathedral, representing Charlemagne on horseback, now in the Louvre, Paris.

The treasuries of episcopal churches and the abbeys, such as those of Angers, Fontanelle, Conques and many others, were enlarged, while during the 9th and the early 10th centuries numerous rich altar tables were made for the churches of Besançon, St-Germain-des-Prés, Auxerre, St Gall, Luxeuil, St Bertin, and St Remy at Rheims. Above all the church treasuries, such as those in the Auvergne, Rouergue and Toulouse district, acquired reliquaries with statues in embossed gold and silver over a wooden body.

The most ancient known to us was presented in 946 to bishop Stephen, abbot of the monastery of Conques and now in the cathedral of Clermont. But the most famous is that of Ste Foy, in the church treasury at Conques en Rouergue. Its date of manufacture is unknown but according to the *Liber Miraculorum Santae Fidis*, it was 'entirely remade' in the year 980. It has been suggested that the head was worked from the statue of some Roman emperor. However, the modelling of the face and the distant fixed gaze of the eyes, in blue glass paste and white enamel, are too much of a piece with the stylistic characteristics of the entire work to support this hypothesis; moreover these features do not contrast with the hieratic air and the almost obsessive idol-like fixity which also appears in the rigidly frontal pose and right-angled treatment of the figure in its seated position on the throne.

Pieces of goldsmith's work of various origin were added at successive periods to this statue: the earrings, a Moslem product of the 10th century; a piece of rock crystal showing the Crucifixion, Lorraine work of 860; a votive crown of the 11th century; fibulas and belt ornaments of the Gothic period. In addition to sacred images such as the Crucifix, which once stood at the entrance to the choir in the cathedral of Le Mans, statues of living people were also made like that of King Lothair, or the one of Solomon, king of Brittany, dating from the second half of the 9th century and offered by him to Pope Adrian II (867-872).

The gradual enrichment and furnishing of the churches led to the creation of many other objects made of gold. The standard box type of reliquary with stands for altars, continued to be made, but new shapes were evolved. Gospel covers, including the outstanding example of 870 known as the Codex Aureus of St Emmeran (Staatsbibliothek, Munich), were enriched with reliefs in precious metals or in ivory: for example the one belonging to the Psaltery of Charles the Bald dating from the years 860-870, in the Bibliothèque Nationale in Paris, has an ivory relief within a copper frame covered with rows of precious stones. This type continued during the Ottonian period—it is to be seen in the binding of Henry II's Sacramentarium (Staatsbibliothek, Munich), and in the one preserved in the treasury at Aachen which shows the Madonna and Child flanked by the Lives of Christ and the Apostles. The Sion Gospels, said to have belonged to Charlemagne, show, within an 11th-century frame of enamelling and precious

44. Reliquary-goblet. Romanesque. Statens Historiska
Museum, Stockholm.

45. Altar frontal in silver gilt. Romanesque. First half of the 12th century. Cathedral of Città di Castello.

44. Reliquary-goblet. Romanesque. Statens Historiska Museum, Stockholm. Almost certainly of German origin, this reliquary is the result of varied and composite elements: the goblet is Roman, the mount on the other hand is 10th- or 11th-century work, while the base and the cover are 12th-century.

45. Altar frontal in silver gilt. Romanesque. First half of the 12th century. Cathedral of Città di Castello. The strong modelling and the predominance of the narrative are typical of Romanesque art. Two rows of panels show incidents in the life of Christ and three figures of saints including St Florido, the protector of the city; in the centre is a mandorla (almond-shaped panel) with Christ in Majesty.

46. Triptych of the Cross. Workshop of Godefroid. Mid-12th century. Ste Croix, Liège. The triptych, produced by the Mosan school, is in embossed copper, gilded and partly enamelled, derived from the Byzantine reliquaries of the True Cross. In the central compartment two angels show the relic, while beneath are the figures of a group of the resurrected; on the wings are the Apostles.

47. Reliquary. Mosan. Second half of the 12th century. Musées Royaux d'Art et d'Histoire, Brussels. In embossed, chiselled and gilded copper, with niello work and enamelling, this reliquary comes from the church of St Servais at Maastricht. From the small arch at the bottom there rises an abbot, to whom two angels show the hand of God; the figures of the angels are linked with greater linear sensitivity to the surmounting frame with its three lobes.

46. Triptych of the Cross. Workshop of Godefroid. Mid-12th century. Ste Croix, Liège.

47. Reliquary. Mosan. Second half of the 12th century.
Musées Royaux d'Art et d'Histoire, Brussels.

stones, an embossed gold figure of Christ dating from the end of the 12th century (Victoria and Albert Museum, London).

Another genre which became increasingly common was a type of flat covering, entirely embossed and usually in silver. An example of this is the reverse side of the Gospel of St Gauzelin, dating from the end of the 10th century (in the cathedral treasury at Nancy) where the symbols of the Evangelists and the Mystic Lamb are framed within simple plant patterns of classical origin.

Among the first creations of Carolinginan goldsmith's work in which human representation appears, the so-called triumphal arch of Eginhardus should be mentioned. Only a drawing of it remains, but this is sufficient to reveal it as one of the most representative works of the school of goldsmiths at the Aachen court. The representation includes a vast iconographic range. The drawing shows a terrestrial globe on which can be seen the history of the redemption and the reign of Christ; within the depth of the arch were figures of two horsemen trampling down the infernal dragon, and on the pilasters were four warriors and four standardbearers with halos; surmounting the arch were embossed representations of the evangelical symbols and, on top, on one of the front façades and on the sides, Christ among the twelve apostles.

The novel and complex nature of the structural presentation and composition, and the freedom of expression indicated by the unusual figures in the arch of Eginhardus, allow us to fit the solitary gold altar to have survived the Carolingian period into a wider panorama of culture and artistic mastery. It is in the basilica of St' Ambrogio in Milan and was carried out by a master goldsmith called Vulvinius and his assistants about the year 835 for bishop Angilbert II (824-859), a Frankish nobleman.

The design of the covering for the four sides of the altar, balanced and neatly divided by wide enamelled cornices, creates an immediate and solemn monumental atmosphere. Since the work served both as an altar and as a reliquary, the decoration necessarily follows two themes and offers us a succession of sacred narratives, as though it were a great cycle presented in sculpture or frescoes; the detail of the panels and frames and of the enamelled decorations, where the bright colouring is reinforced by precious stones and filigree, is extremely small and requires close, attentive study. The panels in embossed silver and gold are from the hands of various artists. Vulvinius is perhaps recognisable in the reliefs on the sides (a jewelled cross between angels and saints) and on the back façade (Stories of St Ambrose) where he is shown in one panel in the act of receiving the crown from the saint himself, designed as a companion piece to the crowning of bishop Angilbert II. The most important collaborator, on the other hand, executed the incidents shown on the front part in gold. Vulvinius expressed himself in sculptural and linear styles of great beauty. Limpid contours define firm shapes in a broad calm pose; in telling the story he isolates the principal fact without indulging in details, but with a few scattered indications of landscape he surrounds the figures with an unreal atmosphere. On the front façade are twelve stories from the New Testament which flank the central cross shape, with its figures of Christ and symbols of the Evangelists and the Apostles. The artist displays a more narrative spirit than Vulvinius and expresses himself in a type of embossed work more tormented and pictorial in spirit, inherited from Byzantine art. Although neither artist can be assigned to one distinct school and although there are stylistic links with Tours and Rheims, both internal and external evidence shows that the work was executed in Milan.

Milan was an important artistic centre. The artists responsible for the altar may well have come from other places, but it would have been natural for them to assimilate such elements of local culture as suited them and also in the broader view, the survivals and echoes of Byzantine culture. It was an ambience moreover conscious of the importance of artistry; apart from the representation referred to above as a companion piece to that of the bishop-donor, there was a later inscription beside the figure of the bishop in which the *magister faber* Vulvinius is described in niello characters exalting the splendour and beauty of this work, which in fact sums up better than anything else the formal perfection, the spirit and the novelty of Carolingian culture, while this is one of the greatest chefs d'oeuvre of medieval Europe. The same cultural environment produced the well known iron crown of Lombardy; this magnificent crown of gold,

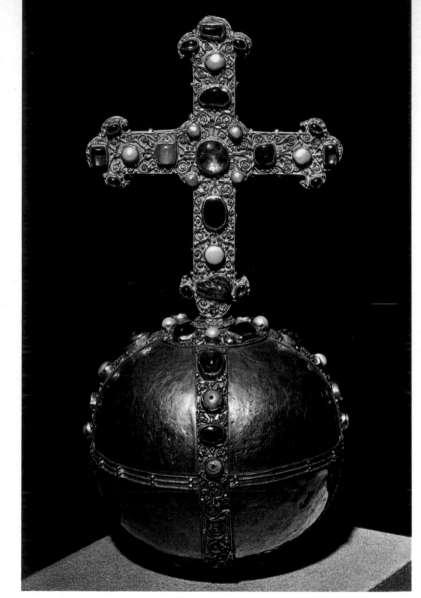

48. Imperial orb in gold and precious stones. Romanesque.
12th century. Kunsthistorisches Museum, Vienna.

49. Ewer in silver gilt. From Lorraine. 12th century. Victoria and Albert Museum, London.

48.   Imperial orb in gold and precious stones. Romanesque. 12th century. Kunsthistorisches Museum, Vienna. In this piece, another symbol of Imperial power, there is particularly outstanding work in gold filigree and seed pearls in the cross and the strips which divide up the orb.

49.   Ewer in silver gilt. From Lorraine. 12th century. Victoria and Albert Museum, London. The workshops in the Rhineland area produced many ewers—this one dates from about 1130 —in the shape of birds or lions; other similar ones were produced later by the workshops at Dinant.

50.   Reliquary. Lower Saxony. c. 1200. Kestner Museum, Hanover. German goldsmith's work of the Romanesque period has qualities of monumental modelling and intense expressiveness which bring it close to the loftiness and originality of the sculpture of that period.

51.   Karlsschrein. German. First quarter of the 13th century. Aachen cathedral. The great chest, made in the shape of a basilica, decorated with about 145 enamels and 400 precious stones, shows, on the side reproduced here, the Holy Roman Emperor between Pope Leo III and archbishop Turpin. The statues, treated completely in the round, have an extraordinary power in their expressive modelling.

50. Reliquary. Lower Saxony. *c.* 1200. Kestner Museum, Hanover.

enamel and jewels, in Monza cathedral, gets its name because it is reinforced inside with a small band of iron which is fastened with a nail believed to be from the True Cross. Although ascribed along with other works at Monza to the time of Queen Theodelinda, the crown is not Lombard in style. The free conception of the ornamentation of the six golden sections, the importance of the embossed work, and the precise analogies in the design and the execution of the enamel all reveal similarities to the altar of Vulvinius, and indeed both works can be ascribed to the 9th century.

There is a clear contrast between goldsmith's work and Carolingian art in other fields, such as the majestic architecture, the grandiose cycle of frescoes at Münster in the Grisons and the serene paintings in S. Benedetto at Malles, the ivories, the incised crystals, the sculpture in bronze and stucco and the flourishing schools of miniature painting.

However the survival of a different style of expression and quality, alien to the coherent discipline of classical art, is illustrated by two objects at Monza. These are the pectoral cross (plate 34), according to tradition given by Queen Berengaria (888-924), and the reliquary of St John the Baptist's tooth, in the form of a purse (plate 33), which can be ascribed to the 9th century. Save for the two young lions on the reliquary, both works are devoid of plastic interest; moreover they lack the high quality of embossing or casting so generally characteristic of Carolingian goldsmith's work.

51. Karlsschrein. German. First quarter of the 13th century. Aachen cathedral.

The goldsmith's interest, obviously, is entirely in the material. The prominence of the Chi-Rho (the monogram of Christ), which dominates in the reliquary, and the exaltation of the relic contained in it are expressed through the material ostentation of the gold and gems. The treatment of the surface as though it were an embroidery is brilliantly executed with the luminous and splendid, unearthly chromatic effects of the gems. Complicated and highly skilled work covers the background with its close designs of ribbon-like gold coils, a line of granulated gold, and seed-pearls, against which the stones blend without a break. The pouch-shape treatment was particularly widespread in the Alpine area and was already known during the third quarter of the 8th century.

Another example is the reliquary from the church of St Dionysus at Enger, now in the Kunstgewerbe-museum, Berlin. On the top are five lions, while against the dark background with its rich coloured effects produced by almandines and cloisonné glass paste stones the basic geometric composition stands out, the Chi-Rho with the thirteen stones placed in a complex cosmological figurative arrangement: the large gem surrounded with pearls in the centre of the cross is the symbol of Christ, and from it the diagonal arms stretch out, to symbolise heaven. The gold-smith's art was intensely cultivated during the Otto-nian period. There were workshops everywhere, in Cologne, Ratisbon, Hildesheim, Fulda, Mainz, and many other places, but above all in Trier. This centre acquired particular importance during the last

52. Circular fibula in gold and precious stones. Rhineland.
13th century. Altertumsmuseum, Mainz.

52.   Circular fibula in gold and precious stones. Rhineland. 13th century. Altertumsmuseum, Mainz. The brooch, in the form of a wheel, is worked in a light but rich openwork design which enchances the opulence of the precious stones in their settings.

53.   Constance of Aragon's coif. 13th century. Palermo cathedral. Apart from embroidery in gold and silver thread, regal and ecclesiastical vestments had enamelling, precious stones and goldsmith's work of various types applied to the fabrics. This headgear, which once belonged to the wife of Frederick II, is decorated with enamelling, precious stones, pearls and also with two long pendants, following a widespread Byzantine fashion.

54.   Altar cross from the abbey of Oignies. Gothic. Second quarter of the 13th century. Victoria and Albert Museum, London. Jewelled crosses are clear examples of the extent to which the symbolic value of gold and gems and their intrinsic worth affected their use, beyond any interest they may have possessed in relation to artistic expression.

55.   Fragment of a reliquary. Mosan. 13th century. Victoria and Albert Museum, London. As early as the 12th century the atmosphere of Mosan work anticipated the modelling of later Gothic art. In this design the treatment of the foliage and of the figures of men and monsters shows a strong stylistic rationality: this is evident in the fullness of the volumes, the lively and fluid movement and the strong dramatic quality which is emphasised by the contrasts of light and shade.

53. Constance of Aragon's coif. 13th century. Palermo cathedral.

54. Altar cross from the abbey of Oignies. Gothic. Second quarter of the 13th century. Victoria and Albert Museum, London.

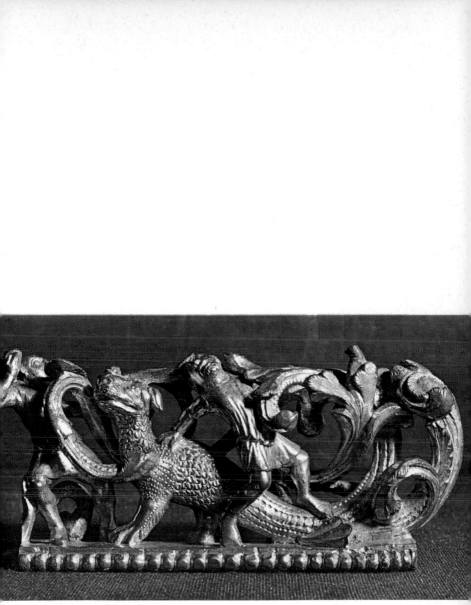

55. Fragment of a reliquary. Mosan. 13th century. Victoria
and Albert Museum, London.

years of the 10th century under bishop Egbert, and its style continued the outstanding harmony of proportion and motif derived from classical antiquity and the widespread use of incised stones. Between the end of the 10th century and the beginning of the next, goldsmiths developed the plastic quality of their work which had acquired a new importance with the Carolingian civilisation. Examples from this period include embossed panels with scenes from the life of Christ such as those in the altar of Otto III (Aachen cathedral); impressive figures of Christ and the saints, as in Henry II's altar frontal in Basle cathedral, now in the Musée de Cluny, Paris; statues in which embossed gold leaf was fixed over a wooden base, like the Mother and Child Enthroned in Essen cathedral. The style of jewelled crosses also became more beautiful and precious; for example the Imperial cross, in the Schatzkammer, Vienna, which shows extremely refined work in pearls with filigree and seed-pearls in gold, or the beautiful cross of Otto and Matilda in the cathedral at Essen dating from 973-982, or the so-called Lothair cross (Aachen) or that from the workshop of Roger of Helmarshausen made in about 1100 (Kunstgewerbemuseum, Berlin). Works in gilt bronze or copper show the same refinement in execution as creations in gold and are often enriched further with openwork and gems.

There is a strong Ottonian flavour about the culture of Milan during the first half of the 11th century, when the city was dominated by the great personality of archbishop Aribert of Intimiano

(1018-1045). From this period date the great Crucifix in embossed gilt copper which is in the cathedral, and the Gospel cover, in the cathedral treasury, of which one side has a faintly archaic air, enriched with magnificent enamelling, and the other has embossed figures with obvious plastic qualities.

THE ROMANESQUE AND GOTHIC PERIOD

Before the Romanesque period the goldsmith's art was practised mainly in the monasteries. The Benedictine Desiderius, abbot of Monte Cassino (11th century) and Suger, abbot of St Denis (11th-12th centuries), renowned for their patronage of the arts in general, were also great patrons of goldsmiths. The priest Theophilus, author of *Diversarum Artium Schedula,* was probably a Benedictine also. His book is a true manual of applied art and gives us much valuable information on the processes used in goldsmith's work during his time. Monasteries, writes Theophilus, are built in such a way as to allow the various arts to be practised; they had places equipped with furnaces, bellows, anvils, tanks, the *organarium* for drawing the gold out into threads, and tools, which constituted the mainstay of the workshop because it was there that work could be carried out by the *'aurifices, inclusores, seu vitrei magistri',* the three branches, that is, of the goldsmith's trade, the man who worked the precious metals, the one who handled and set the gems, and finally the one who carried out the enamelling. Apart from the monastery workshops there are already records in the 12th century of lay workshops, for example the one in Paris where hairpins, necklaces and other articles of personal adornment were manufactured *à l'usage des barons et des nobles dames* ('after the manner favoured by members of the aristocracy').

All the distinguishing characteristics of Romanesque sculpture are found in the goldsmith's work of the period. The new inventiveness of Romanesque sculpture, which is more fruitful, is an inclination towards robust and rapid narrative and towards the representation of a world that is no longer either absorbed in devotion or grandly remote, but dramatic and earthly and human. This tendency is seen even in the rendering of sacred figures, where the aggressive modelling is sometimes severe and grim but always dominant. Nor were extremely precise classical elements alien to this sculptural style, though the influence of other cultural traditions is also evident in varying degrees from one region to another. Indeed, survivals of the most important and dominating of these other traditions, the Byzantine expressive 'manner', can be seen even after the 11th century on embossed gold Gospel covers, reliquaries and enamels.

In southern Italy, for example, 'Greek' painters and mosaic workers were welcomed, and from Byzantium had come the great bronze doors encrusted with silver in the cathedral of Amalfi (1063), the church

56. Onyx cameo representing an eagle. German. Mid-13th century. Schatzkammer, Munich.

58. Medallion in gold and jewels. Gothic. 14th century.
Statens Historiska Museum, Stockholm.

56.   Onyx cameo representing an eagle. German. Mid-13th century. Schatzkammer, Munich. Gem carving was an independent aspect of goldsmith's work. A great number of cameos were produced during the 13th century, and in most of them the design was cut on the light-coloured surface of the stone. Frederick II's collection included hundreds of examples of them, and many were produced for the dignitaries of the court.

57.   Processional cross. Italian. 13th century. Sta Maria presso S. Celso, Milan. This cross in red jasper and silver filigree comes from the abbey of Chiaravalle in Milan. The figures of Christ and the mourners were added during the 16th century, and altogether this work constitutes an anthology of pieces, some of the most important being ten cameos of the 13th century.

58.   Medallion in gold and jewels. Gothic. 14th century. Statens Historiska Museum, Stockholm. The central part, a 14th-century product (possibly from Lübeck), has a wheel motif with jewels and figures; it was added during the 15th century to a gold plaque with eagles and lions.

59.   Reliquary of St Elisabeth. German. 13th century. St Elisabeth, Marburg. This reliquary is closely related to the famous Karlsschrein at Aachen. The sophisticated quality and minute detail of the ornamental motifs are obvious here, while the figures, which are entirely in the round, show a rhythm that is already Gothic in character.

59.   Reliquary of St Elisabeth. German. 13th century. St Elisabeth, Marburg.

of Monte Cassino (1072) and St Michael's chapel at Monte St' Angelo in Apulia (1076). Here, in fact, the current of Byzantine influence continued and was revived in goldsmith's work through steady contacts and the importation of such products as painted ikons in silver frames, and enamels.

The most obvious field in which the new sculptural tendencies of the Romanesque are seen in goldsmith's work is that of small-scale sculpture. Particularly this is so in embossed or cast work, such as the reliquaries in the form of heads, or the embossed altar frontals with framed sets of representational panels, a genre which had already become widespread during the Carolingian and Ottonian periods.

There is the altar frontal given by Pope Celestine II to the cathedral of Città di Castello, his native city, in 1143; it was probably the work of local goldsmiths. The relief is powerfully modelled and the narrative interest handled with imagination, as in the scene showing the flight into Egypt in which St Joseph is almost running with the Christ Child on his shoulders while Mary intervenes, raising her hand as she speaks. As the piece has no enamelling or gems, ornaments or details in gold, the chromatic contrast between the gilding of the faces and the silver background alone distinguishes the one from the other, and attention is concentrated entirely on the sculptural effect. Retables of the late Romanesque and Gothic periods also display close links with sculpture and, like that of St James in the cathedral of Pistoia, also include statuettes cast entirely in the round.

This occurs also in the crosses. The archaic type of cross, in which religious symbolism rather than the human drama of life predominates, was covered with gems as is the 13th-century example from the abbey of Oignies, now in the Victoria and Albert Museum in London. This style continued, but in addition a new interpretation now became prevalent, characterised by applied figures and original colouration, for example the 13th-century cross of Sta Maria in S. Celso, Milan, while a type of processional cross was developed and widely copied throughout the 15th century. Two fine examples of processional crosses are the great cross of Rome and the cross of Andreolo. The great cross of Rome now in the Palazzo Venezia in Rome, dates from 1334 and, with the drapery of its figures, shows a late Gothic sensibility although the outlines of the relief are still firm and stately. The cross of Andreolo de' Bianchi (Sta Maria Maggiore, Bergamo), dating from the last quarter of the 14th century, has a more dynamic outline derived from the rich floral ornamentation which flares out from the arms. The pastoral crosses show small figures, which are closely connected with the curving shapes in which they appear: they were first made in France, but their use spread also to Italy and they were produced in Siena and Umbria.

The 12th and 13th centuries were a period of formal exploration in the regions of the Rhineland and the Meuse. In the 12th century these workshops produced ewers in animal shapes—lions and birds— from the Rhineland workshops, and from about 1215 come ewers in the shape of antique busts crowned with garlands (cathedral treasury, Aachen). Also from the 13th century come the large chests which the enamellers favoured for their decorative potential. The finest of these included the Three Kings shrine at Cologne, designed by Nicholas de Verdun and finished in about 1210; the coffer of Notre Dame at Tournai, dated about 1205; another called the Chest of the Great Relics at Aachen, made before 1238; and finally that of St Elisabeth in the church of that name at Marburg, about 1249, which has a rhythmic quality that could already be described as Gothic. In all these works, as in the delightful group which constitutes the reliquary of St Simeon in the cathedral treasury of Aachen, the human figure dominates in a clearly told narrative.

Perhaps the most outstanding of them all is the great Karlschrein in Aachen cathedral, made about 1200-1215 from silver, gold, enamel work and jewels, which according to tradition contains the remains of Charlemagne. It is in the shape of a basilica, with episodes from the reign of the great king displayed on the embossed panels of the lid, surrounded by a colonnade of arches. A gathering of twelve Carolingian and Germanic kings are assembled on the longer side to watch over the remains of Charles, the Holy Roman Emperor, referred to in the inscription as 'the light and jewel of the Church of Christ, the flower of kings, the ornament of the world'.

The use of enamelling gradually spread in the workshops of the Limousine district, and also in the

60. Processional cross. From Rosciolo in the Abruzzi. Dated
1334. Palazzo Venezia, Rome.

60.   Processional cross. From Rosciolo in the Abruzzi. Dated 1334. Palazzo Venezia, Rome. This unusual type of cross was fairly widespread in central Italy during the 14th and 15th centuries, most of the surviving examples being in the Abruzzi and Umbria.

61.   Detail of Plate 60. The modelling of the figures has here reached a high level of originality, refinement and sensitivity.

62.   Seal of Cividale. Gothic. 1396. Museo Archeologico, Cividale. Gothic seals are outstanding in their stylised linear composition.

63.   Crown. English or French. Schatzkammer, Munich. The crown worn by Blanche, daughter of Henry IV of England, at her marriage to the Elector Ludwig III of Bavaria in 1402. The circular base consists of rosettes in pearls and gems mounted in gold, and from it rise slender and delicate fleurs-de-lys, alternatively large and small; the bezels holding the stones and pearls stand well out and increase the lightness and elegant delicacy of the work.

61.   Detail of Plate 60.

62. Seal of Cividale. Gothic. 1396. Museo Archeologico, Cividale.

63. Crown. English or French. Schatzkammer, Munich.

Meuse and Rhineland area. At first it was still typified by the Byzantine cloisonné work, but later the technique known as champlevé was used, and the enamelling extended over almost the entire surface of the object. Most of the work consisted of church furnishings—reliquary cases, crosses, censers, pyxes, portable altars, bishops' croziers. When copper came into use later, the enamelling became the main vehicle of the artist's expression. Although the representational parts in applied work, which were cast and chiselled separately, reveal taste and a truly sculptural quality, the original beauty of these works is due to the colouring of the enamelwork, which acquires an intense expressive power in the shaded tones used by Godefroid de Huy, or with the neat juxtaposition of turquoise, green and white or red, green and yellow, or red, blue and white characteristic of Limoges. The thin metallic grid structure of champlevé work surrounds the figures, separates the various coloured surfaces, gives a clear outline to agitated dramatic scenes and, while tracing the details of the figures, accentuates the flowing lines. Between the 13th century and the first half of the 15th century goldsmith's work presents original characteristics, which are clearly distinguished from Romanesque taste. Most important are a reasoning type of energy, vertically slanting profiles, studied treatment in which every detail contributes to an effect of extraordinary lightness, an enhancement of the parts with representational modelling and ornamentation, a progressive and continuing search after elegance and refinement, a naturalistic type of interest which seems to tend in some cases towards realistic appearances, and a decorative vocabulary of great magnificence. These characteristics together made a particular 'manner' which goldsmith's work helped to make international.

Gothic art had come to Italy through the influence of the Cistercians, and the style remained predominantly in the north, although encouraged in the south by Frederick II and then by the Angevins. The important Italian centres of Gothic culture were provided by Lombardy and Venice, Tuscany and the Abruzzi, Orvieto and Naples. There were extremely close contacts and exchanges between Italians living in these areas and the high Gothic culture beyond the Alps, exchanges which were not limited to production in gold but also extended to sculpture and painting. In fact these latter increase our understanding of certain changes of taste in some aspects of goldsmith's work. In casting and embossing all possible form of luminous expression were sought, while enamelling became increasingly sophisticated as the degree of translucency of the glass was progressively refined. Siena is a good example of the extension of the Gothic style into Italy. The town had welcomed with equal grace the most grandiose of Byzantine art and the most exquisite products of French Gothic, and occupies an outstanding position in European goldsmith's work of the 14th century. Sienese goldsmiths went to France and Naples where they came to know Gothic products and where, as in England or Spain, their own work became widespread.

Gothic chests were made in the shape of the new chapels and churches, and reliquaries and monstrances in the shape of tabernacles and *tempietti*; reliquary busts, such as the 13th-century example in the Kestner Museum, Hanover, were sometimes highly stylised, while others were so naturalistic as to be almost true portraits. One of the most notable of these is the reliquary bust of St Januarius in Naples cathedral, made between 1304 and 1306 by the French artists Milet d'Auxerre and Guillaume de Verdeley; another splendid Gothic series is in the cathedral of Volterra. The Virgin from the abbey of Roncesvalles and the Virgin of Jeanne d'Evreux (1339) in the Louvre, are true statues even if their dimensions are reduced. The former shows that statues with a wooden base covered with metal foil were still being made in the 14th century, although they had first appeared as far back as the Ottonian period. The latter work is cast and is rich in exquisite details and rhythms in the slightly leaning figure, in the way in which the Child adapts himself to these curves, and in the undulating outline of the drapery.

Statuettes which are cast and often gilded, such as the two angels supporting the casket in the reliquary of St Dominic at Bologna, form important parts of reliquaries. They may contribute to the decoration of the base and the coping, as in the reliquary of the corporal (chalice cloth) in the cathedral of Orvieto, or be found in the crooks of pastoral staffs as part of the narrative (this is especially characteristic of Limoges work though a most beautiful Sienese example can be seen at Città di Castello) or they may weave fine discursive threads in monstrances and altars, for example the altar of St James in the cathedral of Pistoia, or that of St John in the cathedral museum at Florence. They are designed with the sinuous and fan-like movement of fluttering drapery and the delicate grace of composition that pervades the whole of Gothic art.

Chalices, like the Venetian one in the Victoria and Albert Museum in London, were enriched with small figures and scrolls or sometimes with designs in silver which contrasted with the gold background, or with enamelled medallions. Reliquaries and ciboria acquired shapes which resembled with increasing closeness those of buildings or cathedrals or even of facades, always crowned with lofty pinnacles and spires, with climbing leaves and delicate spandrels. In France and Flanders these are found as early as the 13th century; the reliquary of St Taurin, preserved at Evreux, for example, dates from the middle of the century. In Italy the best pieces include the reliquary in copper gilt of St Savino (cathedral museum, Orvieto), made by Ugolino di Vieri in 1338, and the monstrance of Voghera made in 1456 and now in the Castello Sforzesco in Milan.

In Spain, the strong local Romanesque tradition persisted throughout the 13th century, but during the 14th, the workshops of Valencia entered into competition with other European centres, particu-

64. Chalice with blue glass bowl. 15th century. Monza cathedral.

65. Processional cross. Andreolo de' Bianchi. 1392. Sta
Maria Maggiore, Bergamo.

64. Chalice with blue glass bowl. 15th century. Monza cathedral. Although this object is still reminiscent of the transparent Byzantine goblets in crystal or stone mounted on metal, the design of the mount and the proportions are clearly Gothic, as are the shape of the openwork base and the free decoration with foliage and flowers which runs over the knop.

65. Processional cross. Andreolo de' Bianchi. 1392. Sta Maria Maggiore, Bergamo. This cross, in silver gilt, is an example of Gothic elaboration. Notice the refined decoration of enamelling and filigree, the shape of the four-lobed sections, the flowery embroidery surrounding them, and the knop with a small temple complete with cupolas.

66. Reliquary of St Galgano. Sienese. End of the 13th century. Cathedral museum, Siena. Reliquaries and ciboria were made more frequently in the shape of chapels and cathedrals, decorated with tall pinnacles and slender spires. This one was an innovation among the first examples of Sienese goldsmith's work of the Gothic period.

67. Crook of pastoral staff. Sienese. End of the 14th century. Cathedral of Città di Castello. In Umbria Sienese goldsmith's work was particularly influential and was in its turn influenced by French forms. Typically Sienese features are the arrangement of the ornamentation, the refined use of line and translucent enamelling and the extremely beautiful small figures reminiscent of northern European work.

66. Reliquary of St Galgano. Sienese. End of the 13th century. Cathedral museum, Siena.

67. Crook of pastoral staff. Sienese. End of the 14th century.
Cathedral of Città di Castello.

larly with its original style of silver crosses with transparent enamelling. The main altar of the cathedral of Gerona is an important demonstration of the encounter with the new style and its assimilation in a spectacular monumental and architectural achievement. Only the retable and the canopy remain, the Romanesque gold frontal having been melted down in 1806 in order to pay a heavy tribute to the army of Napoleon, but the splendour of the whole conception can nevertheless be envisaged. Work was begun in 1254 but only completed over a century later in 1357, and throughout this long period the gradual resolution of the stylistic conflict went on. The dossal, the work of the goldsmiths Bartomeu, Andreu and Pere Bernec, comprises a vast group of stories and figures on three levels. These include, on the first row beside the Virgin and Child, figures of saints separated by cusps and, in the two succeeding rows, incidents in the life of Christ beneath broader arches and decorated cusps. The skillful deployment of the various materials, gold, silver and enamelling, together with the three slanted crowning tabernacles contribute to the animation of the prevailingly horizontal shape of the retable in the narrative area, and also give that vertical type of movement which the new taste required. The representation of Paradise, with long lines of triumphant saints flanked by tiny figures in prayer like those grouped round the Coronation of the Virgin, is displayed on the front of the silver canopy, supported by slender columns, which dates from about 1350.

In the Low Countries the Mosan (Meuse) school continued to flourish with the work of Hugo d'Oignies, who between 1220 and 1230 developed a type of filigree that was raised off the background sheet metal by means of spirals and vineleaves. England produced large quantities of goldsmith's work, also of large dimensions and often enamelled. In France and Germany relatively few pieces survive which can be attributed to specific masters, but in Italy there are more signed works.

We have the names of the Sienese goldsmiths active during the 14th century at the papal court of Avignon, while it is known that Ugolino di Vieri was responsible for the reliquary of the corporal in the cathedral of Orvieto (1347), and between 1350 and 1357 the Milanese Borgino del Pozzo carried out the altar frontal with the stories from the life of John the Baptist, in Monza cathedral, The altar of St James in Pistoia cathedral has a frontal and a retable divided into rectangular scenes like that of Monza, and the names of the craftsmen who worked on them at various times are known—Andrea d'Jacopo d'Ognabene and Gilio Pisano, followed by Francesco di Niccolò (1361), Leonardo di ser Giovanni (1371), the German Piero d'Arrigo (1381-1394), Nofri di Buto and Atto di Piero Braccini. Craftsmen who worked on the Florentine baptistery included Betto di Geri and Leonardi di ser Cristoforo, and later Cristofano di Paolo and Michele del Monte.

Within the new courtly and privileged society the demand for luxury objects increased. Small enamelled plaques were sewn together with pearls into embroidery for clothes and ceremonial headgear, such as Constance of Aragon's coif in the cathedral treasury at Palermo; a new specialisation grew up in the craft to produce the incised gems for which the demand continually increased.

Paris, where the goldsmiths had formed themselves into a corporation during the reign of Philippa Auguste, rapidly became the major centre of production and in 1292 included at least 120 goldsmiths among its craftsmen.

In men's and women's jewellery, the refined and aristocratic motifs of Gothic art were presented in a particularly magnificent fashion. Splendid jewellery moreover had come to be regarded as a symbol of social prestige; it became accepted and spread widely. Clasps, necklaces, broad gold belts set with pearls and precious stones came into vogue, so that Cacciaguida in the XVth Canto of Dante's *Paradiso,* demands a return to those more austere times when women 'had no necklace, no crown, no close-fitting gown, no belt that was more conspicuous than her own person'.

Jewellery tended to follow the elegant taste which had spread from France to the rest of Europe. Whether it were a small jewel or a complex work on a large scale it would always be dominated by intense colour, the search for luminous effects and the frequent breaking up of the line and heightened chiaroscuro effects. The effect on a large scale can be seen in the 'Pala d'Oro' in S. Marco, Venice, whose frame dates

68.   Monstrance. Lombard. Dated 1456. Castello Sforzesco, Milan. This monstrance from S. Lorenzo in Voghera, is an example of the Gothic forms and architectonic proportions which were very widespread in Lombardy. At the summit is the figure of Christ, and on the knop there are saints on an enamelled background and figures in high relief. These latter, at the base, are the Madonna and Child, a Pietà, St Ambrose, St George and St John the Baptist.

69.   Silver cross. Nicola da Guardiagrele. Dated 1434. Aquila cathedral. This cross, although clearly Gothic in character, shows clear relationships with the Florentine atmosphere, especially with the first door made by Lorenzo Ghiberti.

70.   Chalice. Venetian. Third quarter of the 15th century. Victoria and Albert Museum, London. The decoration adds a note of fantasy to the structure which surmounts it. The relief is fine and delicate, and the linear-type treatments of the separate parts are exquisite. This magnificent chalice is by the same Venetian master who produced the silver gilt candlestick of Doge Moro (now in S. Marco, Venice).

71.   Crown for a sacred image. German. 15th century. Museo Nazionale del Bargello, Florence. The brilliance of the stones is given its full value by the light reflected from the corner-edged mounts.

146

68. Monstrance. Lombard. Castello Sforzesco, Milan.

69. Silver cross. Nicola da Guardiagrele. Dated 1434.
Aquila cathedral.

70. Chalice. Venetian. Third quarter of the 15th century.
Victoria and Albert Museum, London.

from 1345 (see plate 6). This same method of setting the stones, which were still at this period only rounded and not elaborately faceted, was dictated by the need to create refractive angles and reflections. In the 'Pala d'Oro' bezels with sharp corners form the throne of Christ Pantocrator and surround it with a scintillating frame with multiple cusps. Dignitaries, both lay and ecclesiastical, demanded rings, brooches, necklaces, magnificent golden crosses and vestments embroidered in gold and embellished with enamelling and pearls, to exalt both their personal prestige and that of their office.

The most outstanding collection of valuables amassed by any cleric during the 12th and early 13th

71. Crown for a sacred image. German. 15th century. Museo Nazionale del Bargello, Florence.

centuries was probably that of cardinal Guala Bichieri, who in 1219 bequeathed it to his beloved abbey of St' Andrea at Vercelli. It included more than ninety rings, among them fourteen with jacinths and sapphires, nine with single sapphires, eight with emeralds and nine with rubies, many silver crosses, a silver censer and one in Limoges enamelling, vessels and chalices in silver and silver gilt. Numerous other pieces were enclosed in various jewel cases, and two large ones in Limoges enamelling must have formed in themselves chefs d'oeuvre of goldsmith's work. In addition to objects of ritual use (two silver mass-cruets, a gold censer and another in silver, two gold chalices, etc) and gold crosses, there is also a

record of sumptuous table services among which were twenty-three gold and silver cups with covers, four parcel gilt silver bowls, ten gold cups with spiral stems, one in silver, and a gold tray with precious stones.

The most splendid jewels were usually those commissioned for kings: St Louis IX of France (d. 1270), for example, had a reliquary crown in the shape of a lily in which were set a ruby and a fragment from the Crown of Thorns. But members of the aristocracy might own pieces almost equally valuable, and the crowns worn by princes and dukes might often vie with that of the sovereign. Among the most famous examples of Gothic art are the crowns of Princess Margaret of York and Henry II, both in the Schatzkammer at Munich.

Naturally court inventories and bridal trousseaux are full of long lists of jewels. In 1393 Valentina Visconti, the wife of the Duke of Bavaria, took with her to Paris, among other things, thirty-five rings, fourteen clasps, a gold crown with six large and six small flowers made of 312 gems, another crown with six large and six small lilies, and four gold belts. One of the belts included fourteen sapphires, forty-six rubies, thirty-four large pearls, fifty-six diamonds, one hundred and ten ounces of small pearls.

Following the naturalistic tendency of Gothic taste, trinkets might be in the shape of roses, broom, plants, lilies and wreaths of flowers, or sometimes carry armorial bearings and heraldic mottoes such as *Plus hault, Loy autrepasse tout, A bon droit.*

Judging from the few that have survived and those which are shown in miniature in paintings and on tapestries, these works were among the finest examples of goldsmith's work ever produced.

The aristocratic and courtly quality of goldsmith's work runs through the whole of Gothic art. The extreme technical dexterity and the strange and fantastic naturalism produced an incomparable, sometimes almost finicky, elegance; a sophisticated and precious style had evolved to match the worth of the precious metals. Gothic goldsmith's work was like a hothouse plant, enchanting and slightly unreal, subtly perfect and yet slightly artificial. The enchantment and the memory of it lasted for a long time in Europe, even when, as the 15th century progressed, the new ethos of the Renaissance was developing towards the concepts of proportion and reticence against the background of the new rationalism.

LIST OF ILLUSTRATIONS   Page